BECAUSE I LOVE HIM

ASHLEE DONOHUE

BECAUSE I LOVE HIM

This is a Magabala Book

Leading Publisher of Aboriginal and
Torres Strait Islander Storytellers.

Changing the World, One Story at a Time.

First published 2024
Magabala Books Aboriginal Corporation
1 Bagot Street, Broome, Western Australia
Website: www.magabala.com Email: sales@magabala.com
Because I Love Him was previously self-published in 2020

Magabala Books is assisted by the Australian Government through Creative Australia, its principal arts investment and advisory body. The State of Western Australia has made an investment in this project through the Department of Local Government, Sport and Cultural Industries.

Magabala Books is Australia's only independent Aboriginal and Torres Strait Islander publishing house. Magabala Books acknowledges the Traditional Owners of the Country on which we live and work. We recognise the unbroken connection to traditional lands, waters and cultures. Through what we publish, we honour all our Elders, peoples and stories, past, present and future.

Cover design Nada Backovic Designs
Cover image Stocksy, image #2413638, JR Photography
Author image Liza Moscatelli
Printed in Australia by Griffin Press
ISBN (Print) 978-1-922777-88-1
ISBN (ePDF) 978-1-922777-87-4
ISBN (ePUB) 978-1-922777-86-7

A catalogue record for this book is available from the National Library of Australia

Author's Note

Some names have been changed to protect the privacy and identity of persons involved.

All accounts and recollections are solely those of Ashlee Donohue.

To my great-grandmother, grandmother and mother, for paving the path I walk upon, with light.

Ashlee Donohue, is a proud Aboriginal woman from the Dunghutti nation, born and raised in Kempsey, New South Wales. She is an author, educator and media commentator advocating domestic and family violence awareness. Ashlee has created a platform to share lived experiences, as well as a safe place and support network for many women.

Ashlee has appeared on the ABC (*The Drum*), NITV and SBS, and has written for publications such as *Mamamia*, *IndigenousX* and *The Guardian*, and appeared on many podcasts.

A highly sought-after facilitator, speaker, consultant and powerful advocate, Ashlee has presented at the United Nations Commission on the Status of Women forums in New York City. She has been the lead writer and co-creator for numerous anti-violence campaigns and anti-racism education materials, adaptations and reviews of a variety of work.

Ashlee is currently the CEO of Mudgin-Gal Aboriginal Women's Centre, sits on the City of Sydney's Aboriginal and Torres Strait Islander Advisory panel and is on the Domestic Violence New South Wales Aboriginal and Torres Strait Islander Steering Committee.

Contents

Prologue

20 October 1988

Dear Mum,
Goodness … have I got a lot to tell you, and it's not good news either.

I spoke too soon about Dan and Cynthia. He was drinking and went stupid, got into Cynthia and accidently hit Eli. Cynthia put a restraining order out on him. This episode has just made Lara worse. You see, she had moved in with them and was just starting to calm down a bit. That has just made her more stubborn than before. Now she won't do what anyone says. Why … I don't know. I wish you'd come home to sort her out. It's just confusing. I can't put it into words.

Then there's Lucy and Floyd. Floyd's drinking heavily, which upsets Lucy, who just last night tried to take an overdose of Floyd's epilepsy tablets. My God, Mum, I don't know what's happening to this family!

Can you imagine the strain this is all having on Nan? Then there's Pop on one of his drinking binges. Nan keeps saying he's going to be the death of her. Things keep going this road and they will.

Oh Mum, this is so sad – our beloved dog Roman accidently hung himself last night. Floyd tied him up at the back fence because he's been running out onto the road chasing cars. When we woke this morning, we couldn't see him. Floyd went down to check on him and found him hanging by his chain on the other side of the fence. He must've jumped over then walked around through the gap in the fence and jumped over again. This upset Nan and poor Eli. Floyd and Lenny buried him over in the bushland near the park and put roses from Nan's garden on his grave. If it doesn't rain it pours.

The only little bit of good news is that Mimi had a baby boy. He's lovely.

Nan, Dave, Tina and I were in the labour ward. She did well. He weighed 7 pounds 14 ounces, measured 22 inches and he's gorgeous! He looks like Lenny and Eli mixed up. She named him Cayne David Mathew Sean after his dad Dave and Uncle Matt. That's the only good news I have. Apart from that everything and everyone else are okay.

But I do wish you'd come home from England. Everyone seems to listen and take notice of you. Oh, dear Mum, now that you've told me you're not well, God love me, I'll probably have a nervous breakdown.

Dan reckons he's going to come after Cynthia and me and drag us around by our hair. I don't know what I've got to do with any of it. Another worry.

Please write a letter to Lara. My baby sister really needs her mother right now. Being sixteen can be hard, Mum. You know that.

Come home soon!

Love,

Ashlee Zenna Dianne xxx

One
Humble Beginnings

The local welfare lady, known as Sister Griffiths, sent my mother to Sydney at the age of fifteen to clean houses. My grandparents (Nan and Pop) lived on the outskirts of Kempsey, New South Wales, and couldn't afford to send her to school. Up to that time, my mother had lived in a tin shack with a dirt floor in the bush on the banks of the Hat Head Creek.

She travelled by herself on the train to Sydney, where she was greeted by a Jewish couple at Central Station. She was then taken to the North Shore to clean a 'very flash house', as she put it, which was probably a mansion – not that she knew what a mansion was back then. She cleaned that house for the princely sum of eight dollars a week. It was 1968.

My mother told me how homesick she was there, how she had no one to talk to or to comfort or support her, so on a rare day off she headed over to a well-known gathering place for Aboriginal people known as the Block, which was in the heart of Redfern, to see if she could find any of her family. It was there that she bumped into her cousin Emmy, who had also grown up in Kempsey. Mum told Emmy what had been going on. Emmy, in turn, informed her that it was slave labour, as her employers had my mother working from 7am until midnight on most days. Emmy told Mum to go and get her things, and to make sure she got her eight dollars too, and that she could stay with her and some other cousins just up the road in Surry Hills.

Mum did as she was told and before long she was living with her cousins. It was there in the heart of the city that my mother became 'acquainted' (as she puts it) with my father, Michael, a twenty-two-year-old brewery worker, over the back fence of the house she shared with her cousins.

As my mother told me, "It was a 'hi' here and a 'hi' there, and 'how're things going?'" until the Easter long weekend. It was Good Friday, and Michael invited my mother and her cousins over for a barbecue. My mother told me with a dry laugh, "I had my first taste of beer, among other things, that night." She also said I was the result of her first and only sexual encounter with my father, on that particular Good Friday. When my mother told him she was pregnant, his response was, "Well I can't marry you, I am already married." She rarely saw him after that.

Once she discovered she was pregnant, my mother would drop in to see her Aunty Polly in Alexandria after each of her doctor's appointments. After her six-month appointment, Aunty Polly became concerned when she found out my mother was to give birth to me at Crown Street Women's Hospital. Aunty Polly warned her that Crown Street Women's Hospital was notorious for taking babies away from their mothers with or without their consent, especially from unmarried Aboriginal women whose babies' fathers were white men. Aunty Polly demanded that Mum return home to Kempsey to deliver me, and gave her money to buy a train ticket. Mum listened to her advice and left the next day.

My name is Ashlee Zenna Dianne Donohue. I was born on 31 December 1968 in a town called Kempsey, the first child born to Patricia Donohue, a sixteen-year-old Aboriginal woman from the Dunghutti Nation, on the mid north coast of New South Wales.

I have one sister – her name is Lara. She's four years younger than me. When I was born, Mum's room was on the Veranda Ward – a zone set aside for Aboriginal women. It was just that – a veranda with mesh around it, segregated from the obstetrics unit and the main maternity ward where the white women stayed.

Mum told me on numerous occasions that the nurses fussed over me because I was such a pretty baby. It was probably because I was blonde haired and blue eyed.

My first home was the same tin shack on the banks of the Hat Head Creek that my mother had left just over a year before, located about forty minutes drive east of Kempsey. My first bed was a bamboo fishing basket. My pop painstakingly washed that basket and filled it with fresh straw and pillow stuffing for my arrival home. In this shack lived Pop, Nan, my mother and six of her brothers and sisters ranging from six months to fourteen years old. There were other shacks in the camp occupied by other family members, including my pop's brother, his wife and their children.

We lived there until I was about two years old, and then the family moved into town because Pop got a job with Kempsey Shire Council. We were one of the first Aboriginal families in the area. Besides us there was Aunty Beryl, an elderly Aboriginal lady who lived by herself across the road, as well as Harriet, who lived with her husband and four children next door. We didn't know her when we arrived, but she became 'Aunty Harriet' over the years.

Pop worked hard and he always provided for us. He was a tall, strong man with distinct Aboriginal features – a handsome man. People would look at us funnily when I would sing out 'Pop' to him in public. Firstly, this was because I looked white, and secondly, because he didn't look old enough to be a grandfather. In actual fact, he wasn't my biological grandfather – he was my biological uncle. He was, however, the only father I knew, and he treated me like one of his daughters.

During my early years, I would travel back and forth with Mum from Kempsey to Sydney quite often. The earliest childhood memory I have from around the age of four or five is of tickling people's feet during prayer time at the Hare Krishna Temple in Glebe. I also remember how delicious the apricot sweets were – little balls of sweet, soft, sticky apricot heaven that would melt in my mouth. I'm not sure what they were made from, but gosh they were scrumptious.

In 1978 my mum moved Lara and me from Kempsey to Sydney. We stayed at her friend Dani's house in Allambie Heights on the North Shore along with Dani's boyfriend, Mick. Mum enrolled us into the local primary school. I was so excited to be going there. I went shopping with Mum and Lara for new school shoes at the St Vincent de Paul Society shop, or Vinnies, and found a perfect brown pair I loved. I thought I was going to fit in.

I settled into school really well. My early days were great. I loved learning and felt really comfortable at the school. I was a happy girl and made friends quite easily.

One of those friends was a girl named Ebony, who I met on the first day. At the time I thought, *Gosh she's perfect.* Later on, I was invited to her house after school where we had biscuits and milk. We walked to school together and played together. She was my first best friend. I wanted to be just like her. I asked Mum if Ebony could come to our house, but Mum said no. I wasn't sure why.

One day at school, we had to do a test. I did it with ease and was so very proud of myself. That afternoon, Dani and her boyfriend Mick came to pick me up from school. I walked out with my teacher Miss Jane holding my hand, but as soon she saw Dani's boyfriend she let go of my hand.

I recall feeling uneasy, but I had no idea why. There was something going on between Mick and Miss Jane, but I was too young to understand.

The next day, Miss Jane's attitude towards me changed profoundly. She accused me of cheating on my test and I had to do it again. She took me into a separate room and made me sit down to do a different test. She sat across from me, glaring. I was so intimidated and scared that I couldn't think straight, and of course I failed.

She then arranged for Mum to come to a parent-teacher meeting. I was so excited when I saw Mum walk through the gates. She looked so pretty with her natural afro, nose ring and a long, flowing, hippie wrap-around skirt with little bells that tinkled on her belt. I ran up to her singing out, "Mummy! Mummy!" and threw my arms around her waist, giving her a big cuddle. I was so happy.

Miss Jane seemed a little shocked when Mum introduced herself as Ashlee's mother. Looking back, she may have thought I was Dani's child.

The next day, barely any of the other children spoke to me, not even

Ebony. I couldn't understand why and felt sad and confused. Then I heard the kids whispering among themselves, "Did you see her nose? She had an earring in it!" and chanting that I was 'dirty' because Mum was black. I'd never noticed that my mother looked a little different. I thought all Mums looked like mine.

After that, the kids didn't want to sit near me. Even Ebony behaved differently towards me and she soon stopped asking me to go over to her place. I felt miserable. This was the first time I realised I was different because I was Aboriginal. I was confused and didn't know how to act or what to do to make everything go back to how it was. It instilled in me a sense of not belonging, as well as the belief that I was not good enough. It was awful.

I went home and cried to Mum. At first, she tried to explain to me that some people reacted to Aboriginal people like this and then she announced, "That's it. We're going home!" We promptly packed up and left Sydney. We were only there for six months.

We moved back to Nan and Pop's house in Middleton Street, Kempsey, which was a four-bedroom weatherboard house. I continued to be raised with my aunties and uncles – six were older than me and four were younger. We grew up more like brothers and sisters than uncles, aunties and niece, and I never actually called them aunty or uncle.

I loved South Kempsey and being with my family. I didn't really need to make friends at school because I had so many relatives there. My school days were filled with happy memories. When I was eleven years old, I was chosen to attend a camp at Stewart House in Sydney. I thought I was selected because I was doing well at school – I had no idea it was a program for disadvantaged kids. It was the first time I had travelled on my own; I was scared and excited at the same time. We had so much fun, with trips to Taronga Zoo, Luna Park and other places that I had never been to before. There were also daily activities like painting and games.

For the most part, my childhood was filled with happiness and love, with flashes of sadness, despair, pain and disbelief. There was a fair bit of drinking at home in Kempsey. Our aunties and uncles would visit occasionally, and they'd all have a drink and then start fighting. At times, we could have up to forty people crammed into our place.

When I was about thirteen years old, a few of the girls decided to sneak out with one of our female cousins whose boyfriend was catching the late train to Armidale. I didn't want to go but my older Aunty Mimi forced me. She grabbed my arm and twisted it, and threatened to hit me if I didn't go with them. I was too scared of her to say no. We placed clothes and pillows under our blankets to make it appear as if we were still there, and turned on the radio. We also put knives in the door, which Nan had previously told us to do when we had a lot of visitors. This was a simple security measure to alert us if anybody tried to sneak into our room while we were sleeping. On this occasion, we put the knife in the door to keep Nan out.

When we were ready, we jumped out the window. We walked to the train station in the dark and then waited for the train to arrive. I was fidgety and kept wishing that the train would hurry up. Then I saw my cousin and her boyfriend kiss … I mean really kiss. It was the first time I'd ever seen anyone kiss. I was mesmerised. Aunty Mimi bumped me and gave me the look – the one that means 'stop staring'. I kept thinking, *I can't wait for a boy to kiss me like that.*

We decided to head home as the train was taking too long, and we left our cousin with her boyfriend. As we walked home, we heard Nan's whistle, followed by the sound of our car – which we had lovingly named Red Back because it was red. We ran and hid in the bushes, but it was too late. We had been spotted and we knew we were going to get it.

The car pulled up and Nan and Pop got out. Before they even came near me, I started crying, "Mummy, Daddy, Mummy, Daddy, no!" No matter what, if any of us kids were in trouble we would always cry, "Mummy, Daddy, Mummy, Daddy!" I'm not sure why – we just did!

Then I thought I could escape from my pop by running away, but I couldn't. He pulled me to the ground by my hair and whacked me with a stick. Except for my cousin, who was still on the train platform, we all got a hiding that night. I never jumped out the window again.

Kempsey was a great place to grow up. We walked everywhere, ran across the train tracks, climbed big trees, played in the park and regularly went to the beach. To this day, Hat Head Creek holds a special place in my heart. I often go there when I'm feeling overwhelmed and stressed. It's my favourite place in the world.

Not long afterwards, my world changed dramatically when two of my aunties (one aged fourteen and the other sixteen) fell pregnant. As a result, my life became restricted. Overnight, I gained a bodyguard in the form of my mother, who accompanied me out at night whenever I went to the blue-light disco. I couldn't understand why. After all, the blue-light disco was organised and overseen by the police. What on earth was I going to do when the police were everywhere and supervising everything?

My mother's minding activities were not just restricted to the disco. No matter where I went, I had to be dropped off and picked up at a scheduled time. It was a bit much, to say the least. It was like I was being punished for their behaviour.

High school was a happy place for me, although I struggled – not so much with the schoolwork but with the exams. I still believe my earlier experience of being labelled a cheat negatively affected my learning, to the point where my Year 10 supervisor advised Mum that it would be a waste of time for me to go on to Years 11 and 12. I remember my mother glaring at him and stating firmly, "She'll be fine!" – and I was.

I got along with most people in high school and had a few best friends who weren't family. I participated in sports, even though I wasn't very good at them. I was often put in the goal defence position for netball because I was tall. I wasn't particularly artistic either, but I was good at reading and talking. I was often expressing my opinion. I had a voice and I wasn't afraid to use it; in fact, I may even have been a little loud.

My first real achievement came when I was sixteen years old. I was in Year 11 when I was asked to participate in a deportment class in Sydney run by the famous June Dally-Watkins. I had decided to be an air hostess (the name for a flight attendant back then) and was told this course would help me achieve that dream by teaching me how to walk, talk and eat in public. June Dally-Watkins was one of the oldest deportment schools in Australia. I took part in the personal development course, which was designed to build confidence and to teach good manners and the value and importance of self-worth and happiness.

I was excited and scared at the same time. I was also ecstatic that my Aunty Cynthia was coming too. We were very close, so this was perfect. We stayed at the YWCA in Sydney. The course went for one week. We learned how to walk properly, how to eat soup, how to use cutlery and how to take care of our hygiene, among other things. It ended with a fashion parade. I really enjoyed it. It was a simple program, but it had an enormous impact. I believe it instilled a little bit of pride in me.

~

I only had one boyfriend during my teenage years, and that relationship lasted for six months. I was fifteen and he was seventeen. He had the loveliest smile and shiny dark skin. His name was Simon.

Simon was the first boy I kissed – and the first to hit me.

I thought I loved him. He was drinking one night at the skate park and then started a fight with me. He pushed me and then punched me in the arm and leg. I couldn't understand why he would do this. I still can't.

I thought we had broken up because of this, I begged Aunty Cynthia to go on a seven-kilometre bike ride with me all the way from our home to North Street to see if he was still my boyfriend. I thought I must have done something wrong for him to want to punch me.

When we finally arrived, I went into his room. He tried to ignore me so I asked him if we were still together. He looked at me shyly and muttered, "Yes, we are."

I threw my arms around his neck, gave him a quick kiss and ran outside as quickly as I could to where Aunty Cynthia was waiting for me. I jumped on the bike and said, "Let's go home."

Aunty Cynthia asked me whether I was okay and I said, "Yep, never been better," then started pedalling. I was terrified Simon would run out of the house after me to say he had changed his mind. As we got further away from his house, I relaxed and smiled all the way home.

We split up two weeks later.

I didn't have another boyfriend for several years after Simon, although I fell deeply and madly in love with one of the new boys who came to our high school in Year 12. His name was Brad, and he was tall with piercing blue eyes and dark brown hair, as well as the muscliest arms I had ever seen. Our friendship blossomed quickly, and there was lots of flirting and swift touching of hands and faces. Then one day he asked me to go to his place. I said, "Yeah sure," as he lived only a five-minute walk away from the high school.

We walked into his house. His mum was on the lounge and he gave her a kiss and introduced me. I thought, *Wow! Isn't he sweet? He still kisses his mum.*

We went into the kitchen, and then he grabbed my hand and took me into his room. He pulled me close and kissed me like I'd never been kissed before. My knees went weak and I saw stars, in a good way. Luckily he had his strong arms around me because I swear I would have otherwise crumbled to the floor. I made the naive assumption that he would have felt as wonderful as I did while experiencing this kiss. As it turned out, that was the first and last time we kissed because he had a girlfriend.

When I turned eighteen I left home and moved to Port Macquarie to live in a big house by the beach with my Auntys Angie and Claudia, and cousins Karen and Ellen. I secured myself a traineeship with a travel agency and my adulthood began.

Two

Love at First Sight

I first met Ronny in May 1990. I was twenty-one years old and felt confident I was on the right track. I had a job, a great group of friends, and I was happy and content.

I was working for the Australian Taxation Office (ATO) in Parramatta. It was my job to track taxation cheques cashed by those who received returns. I had just moved out of the Tony Mundine Hostel in Burwood, along with my Aunty Halle and friend Samantha, to a house in Bexley North in Sydney. It was a lovely little three-bedroom house with a nice backyard. We all settled in well.

Our favourite place to go out in Sydney was a bar called the Clifton in Redfern. It was the place to be – all the Blackfullas used to go there. It was so much fun.

One night, I was flirting with one of the bartenders, who I knew had a crush on me, when someone tapped me on the shoulder and said, "Hey, Ash, I want you to meet my mate Ronny."

I turned around, glanced at Ronny and said, "Hi," and then promptly went back to flirting with the bartender. As the night progressed, my Aunties Halle and Tina along with our cousin Macy ended up at a pub called Mansions in Kings Cross. We walked through the door and our favourite song was playing: 'I Wanna Dance with Somebody' by Whitney Houston. We all started singing, and as I glanced across the room to the pool table there was Ronny holding a pool cue, ready to take his shot.

Our eyes met, and this time I got a good look at him. He was a tall, strapping young man with broad shoulders. His jet-black hair shimmered under the light. His skin was silky black, his eyes piercing brown and his teeth … well, I had never seen anyone with teeth as perfect as his. He was so handsome.

I smiled at him, and he smiled back and nodded his head. I looked away, nudged my Aunty Halle and quietly said to her, "Gee, he's lovely." Then I asked her, "Is he lovely?"

She replied with a giggle, "Yes, yes, he is."

"I bet I can get him," I giggled back.

We walked up to the bar and I told the girls that I was going over to watch the pool players. They looked at me and said in unison, "You don't even like pool."

I gave them a 'whatever' look, walked over to the pool table and propped myself up on a stool so I could get a better look at Ronny.

He turned to me and asked, "You wanna play?" I shook my head and replied, "No, I can't."

He said, "Come on, I'll teach you."

He then gave me the most beautiful smile I had ever seen in my life. His teeth were so white and straight. I couldn't stop looking at them. I think I fell in love that very moment.

I considered his offer for about three seconds and then thought, *Why not*? I walked over and put a twenty-cent coin on the pool table to indicate I was in line to play. Ronny smiled at me again and I blushed.

I sat on a stool and continued to watch him play while cheering him on, chatting away and hoping he would win so I could play with him next. As he sunk the last ball to win the game, I gave out a little, "Woo hoo." I was excited – maybe a little too excited – that he had won.

It was now my time to play. Quite simply put, I was shocking! Ronny tried his best to teach me, but I ended up sinking the black ball and it was all over.

Ronny and I then went and sat down together and chatted for a while. We were squeezed up close, and nobody else existed in that moment. Before I knew it, it was closing time.

My Aunty Halle and cousin Macy came over to collect me to go home. We had a rule when we went out: when one went home, we all went home – no questions asked. I stood up to leave, looked at Ronny and said, "See ya. It was nice meeting you."

He nodded, and then asked if he and his mate could get a lift to Central Station as they were heading back home to Collarenebri. I looked at the girls and they agreed, so we all walked out together, hailed a taxi and dropped the men off at the train station. Just before Ronny got out of the taxi, he kissed me ever so slightly on the lips. I swear my heart missed a beat. Then he and his mate jumped out, waved goodbye and were gone. I thought that was the last I'd ever see of him.

We reached home still buzzing. Macy jumped into bed with me and we giggled as we recapped the night. Samantha was rousing on us for making noise because she had to go to work a few hours later. We continued having a little yarn, then settled in and dozed off.

A short while later, I was woken up when I heard Samantha shouting, "Who the hell are you?"

The voice replied, "It's Ronny, I'm looking for Ashlee."

I sat upright in shock just as Samantha came in and turned on the light.

Samantha asked, "Ashlee, do you know a fulla named Ronny?" "Yes," I said as Ronny casually strolled into my room. I sat up clutching the sheet to cover my mouth because I was trying not to laugh at Samantha – she was so angry. Ronny began to explain how he had missed the train and remembered our address, and then asked if he could stay the night. I asked him how he got in.

He said the key was in the door, which I later found out was true as Aunty Halle had accidentally left the key in the door.

For reasons still unknown to me, I allowed him to stay. Macy jumped up and went into Samantha's room, and Ronny's and my love affair well and truly began. I often joke that I believe I fell pregnant that very morning.

We saw each other every night from then onwards. Our lovemaking was inexperienced, but intense. We kissed so much that our lips became cracked and sore, and he held me in his arms every night as we fell asleep. He was warm, sweet and so handsome. I remember watching him sleep, thinking about how beautiful he was and that I wanted to have his babies.

It was always my intention to have children with a dark-skinned Aboriginal man. I wanted to 'put the black back' into my future babies so they would never have to go through what I did being a fair-skinned Aboriginal person.

About two weeks into the relationship, Ronny was rummaging through his bag and asked me if I'd like a photo of him. I promptly said, "Yes, of course."

When he pulled out his school photo, I nearly choked. "How old are you?" I asked.

He replied, "Seventeen."

I snapped at him, "You told me you were twenty-one!"

He had a full chest of hair. Trying to rationalise the situation, I thought, *What teenager has a full chest of hair?*

I also found out his real name was Aaron, Aaron Stone to be exact. Ronny was his nickname!

For a moment, and only a fleeting moment, I thought about telling him to leave, but I didn't and he stayed.

One night at the Clifton he asked me to go outside with him and proceeded to tell me that he had to go home to Collarenebri that night. I was sad. He gave me a passionate kiss, held me tight and then jumped into a car. I watched him drive away and wondered if he would look back. He did, and this made me happy.

Our love affair lasted for twenty-one days.

The following weeks went by quickly, until one morning I started feeling sick. I popped into the Aboriginal Medical Services to find out what was wrong. The doctor asked whether it was possible I could be pregnant.

I replied, "No way! I'm on the pill."

The doctor said, "Let's take some blood tests just to be sure then, eh?"

After my blood sample was taken, I felt a little scared, hoping I wasn't pregnant. Then, when the girls and I went out later that night, I got my period. It was such a relief.

The following Wednesday I received a phone call from the doctor notifying me I was indeed pregnant.

"No, I'm not. I got my period," I said.

"I'm very sorry, but you are," she replied, and asked if I would like to schedule some more blood tests and an ultrasound for the following week.

I whispered weakly, "Yes, okay."

I put down the phone and felt the blood rush from my face. I thought I was going to faint. My first thought was, *Oh my God! What's Mum going to say?* I felt confused and began to cry. I somehow still didn't believe I could be pregnant.

That thought vanished a few days later when I saw the little dot on the ultrasound and was advised that I was seven weeks pregnant, and the embryo had nestled in tightly.

I walked out of the medical centre with my little photo and felt even more confused than when I walked in. I was going to have a baby. I was scared. My mother was overseas at the time. What was I going to do?

It so happened that the next day, Mum arrived home from her trip. She walked in, put down her bag, came to cuddle me, and I blurted out: "I'm pregnant!"

"What?" she asked.

"I'm pregnant," I repeated and burst out crying. Mum fell back like someone had hit her in the stomach.

Her first questions were, "Who's the father?" and "How far along are you?"

I told her about Ronny and that I was seven weeks pregnant.

The blood drained from her face. She decided to lie down to get a grip on her jet lag, but later had more questions for me. "Where is he? Does he work? How old is he?" and so on.

I told a few white lies. I didn't tell her his age or that he had just left boarding school.

Mum accompanied me to my next doctor's appointment. The doctor and Mum proceeded to ask me what my intention was. I felt as though they were pressuring me to terminate, but I was adamant that I was keeping my baby.

My pregnancy progressed quickly. I had no complications and worked until I was eight months pregnant. The only thing that bothered me was the knowledge that my baby would not know his or her father if I didn't take steps to remedy the situation. The fact that I did not know where the father was didn't help. I hadn't seen Ronny since the annual Aboriginal Rugby League Knockout (the Knockout) in Walgett earlier that year. We spoke briefly and he came and spent the night with me. It was then when I first felt my baby move, and I was overwhelmed with emotion that

Ronny was there to experience it with me. He left the next morning, but I caught up with him later that day and had a photo taken of him so my baby would at least know what his father looked like. I didn't see him again after that.

Having grown up without knowing my father, I was steadfast in the position that my children would know who their father was. I decided to track Ronny down, as I knew his name and the town he was from.

I rang the police station in Collarenebri and asked if they knew Ronny. Luckily, they did. They said the best way to get in contact with him was through his uncle, because he was on a good behaviour bond and under his uncle's supervision. They gave me an address and told me to attention my letter to his uncle.

After hearing this news about Ronny, I became concerned. For a moment I questioned my motives and whether I should bother or not. That thought soon passed. The desire for my unborn child to know his father was much greater than finding out Ronny was on a good behaviour bond.

I wrote Ronny a letter reminding him of his impending fatherhood. I explained that I didn't expect him to do anything, nor did I want anything from him, I just wanted him to be on our baby's birth certificate. Weeks passed by with no reply. I wrote another letter begging him to sign the birth certificate, explaining how I didn't want my child to grow up with a dash beside the father's name like I had or, worse still, have the words 'father unknown' scrawled on there. I received no answer.

It was time to move home to Kempsey to live with my nan. I needed to be near her and have her advice, support and love, so I filled my thoughts with preparing for the birth of my baby.

I settled back home easily, made all the necessary arrangements required for the birth, and sat back and waited.

On 14 February 1991, Valentine's Day, I awoke feeling like I needed to go to the toilet. I sat up and felt like I had wet my pants. I lay back down and it stopped. I sat up again only to encounter more fluid.

I went to the bathroom to discover there was no toilet paper, so I sang out to my pop who said, "I'll go get some from next door if you iron my work shirt."

I agreed. My Aunty Angie lived next door with her partner Bryce and daughter Brittney.

As soon as Nan woke up I said to her, "I think something's going on, Nan."

She asked whether I had any pain or whether there was any 'show'.

I explained there was no pain and asked, "What is show?" She explained to me that it was mucus mixed with blood and that it was "like the plug being pulled from a bath, except it's from your baby." I screwed up my face and told her there was no show.

"Well, nothing's going to happen until you see that," she replied.

I told her I thought my waters had broken, but she repeated that until we saw the show, nothing was going to happen. I believed her ... after all, she did give birth to fourteen children. Nan then told me to go for a walk, so my Aunty Tina and I went for a stroll to the shop. All of a sudden, I had the biggest jolt of pain that I had ever felt (or so I thought at the time). We turned to walk back home and just as we arrived, my Uncle Barney pulled up. I asked him to take me to the hospital. Aunty Tina ran inside to get Nan, and then Uncle Barney bundled us into his car and drove us to the hospital. As he cruised along whistling away with his arm outside the window, I could have sworn that he hit every bump on the road!

I was taken to the maternity ward, where the nurse checked me over and told me I was only two centimetres dilated, so I wouldn't be giving birth any time soon. They told me to go home. "But I think my water broke," I replied. They again instructed me to come back when I had a showing, and so the fun began.

I called Mum and told her I was in labour. She said, "Don't have that baby until I get there!" Guess what? I didn't.

We returned to the hospital at eleven in the morning because I was crying and in agony. I kept asking God why he was punishing me and asking the nurses for drugs. I begged Nan to help me, but her response was, "You wasn't asking for my help when you were making the baby."

The doctor came and checked me and said if I didn't have the baby within twenty-four hours, I would need to have a caesarean. Thankfully, I didn't need to as the baby decided to make an appearance after what I can only describe as a traumatic birth. I was offered no pain relief other than gas. I tried it once and didn't like it. Nan, however, seemed to enjoy it because she kept showing me how it worked by putting the mask over her face and inhaling.

I gave birth to the most beautiful baby I had ever seen. I fell in love with him immediately. It was truly love at first sight. As soon as my son was born, he was placed on my chest and Nan cut his cord. He was perfect, although still a little too white for my liking. After all, I had envisaged a little Black baby with lots of hair! But it didn't matter. All I could do was look at his perfect face and cry. I couldn't believe I had created something so sublime. I asked one of the nurses if this feeling was normal. She said it was and that it was natural to feel overwhelmed with love. I named my baby Axil. I couldn't help but wish Ronny had been there to see him.

Three

Baby Daddy

I settled into motherhood easier than I imagined. However, Ronny was still on my mind, especially since I had to fill out the birth registration forms for our son. I decided to write him another letter. I vowed to myself that this would be the last time I would try to contact him. I sent a photo of Axil, and provided his name and birth details including date, time, weight and length, along with details of how to contact me if he wished.

Another two weeks went by. I was beginning to lose hope when, out of the blue, a woman called me from Collarenebri and said, "I have someone here who wants to talk to you."

It was Ronny. My heart raced. My eyes welled up with tears as he began to speak.

"Hello Ash," he said quietly.

"Hey, Ronny, I'm so glad you called," I replied, holding back tears.

He asked how I was and how the baby was doing. It was a little awkward. I didn't quite know what to say, and neither did he.

Then I blurted out, "Why didn't you answer my letters?"

There was a long pause and then he simply said, "I don't know."

The tears now began to sting my eyes as I mumbled, "You didn't think he was yours, did you?"

He didn't answer.

Logically, I could hardly blame his doubt – we had only been together for three weeks. Emotionally, I felt like saying, *How could you not at least have reached out?* We'd barely spent a moment apart during that time. I was sure that I loved him and my feelings were real, so shouldn't his have been as well?

After that call, we started talking regularly on the phone, and he asked if I would go to Collarenebri.

"No ... you. You come to me," I said. He said he would see what he could do.

My friend Bobby, who I worked with at the ATO, came to see my son and me. As it turned out, he just happened to be on his way to Walgett that weekend. I thought it was destiny because Walgett was only an hour away from Collarenebri.

I told Bobby about Ronny, and how his family wanted me to bring Axil to see them. Bobby then suggested, "Come with me. I'll drop you off in Collarenebri and pick you up on Monday, no worries." I agreed, and called Ronny to let him know I'd decided to visit him. This would be the first of many times I would succumb to his requests, when in reality I should have been resisting and he should have been making more of an effort. A few days later we set off to meet my baby's daddy.

I didn't realise how far away Collarenebri was. It took us nine hours to get there, and my poor baby had never travelled so far in a car. In fact, neither had I. I was becoming progressively uncomfortable with every passing kilometre, and was exceptionally restless towards the end of the trip. I started wondering what on earth I was doing. I really should have made him come to us!

We arrived at Collarenebri just on dark and pulled up outside the address Ronny had given me. I could feel my heart racing as Bobby turned to me and asked, "Are you alright?" I gave him a little nod as I looked at the big white house with a veranda all the way around it and saw people coming to greet us. The first person was Ronny.

I was surprised at how happy he looked and I couldn't help but smile with relief. As he opened the car door for me, I could smell alcohol on his breath. My heart dropped with disappointment.

"Couldn't you stay sober?" I asked quietly, so nobody could hear me.

Ronny's cousin and her parents, brother, sister and daughter welcomed me when I stepped out of the car. They were all lovely and very friendly as they quickly ushered us inside.

Bobby had a cup of tea and a quick yarn, and then I escorted him back to the car.

He asked me again with concern in his voice, "Are you alright?"

"Yeah, I'll be fine," I said. "It's only for the weekend." He smiled and replied, "Okay, see you Monday."

I walked back inside the house and into the lounge room, which they had fixed up for us to sleep in. There was a big open fire, and it was so cosy and warm. Everyone had gathered in and was lining up to nurse Axil. I felt an overwhelming sense of belonging – not for me, but for my son. This warmed my heart, and still does when I think about it to this day.

Eventually everyone went to bed and only Ronny, Axil and I remained in the lounge room. Under the light of the flickering fire, I saw Ronny staring at me.

"What?" I asked.

"Nothing. Just looking at how pretty you are," he replied.

I blushed and gave him a quick smile. It felt so good as he wrapped his strong arms around me when we lay down to sleep. As I dozed off, I could feel tears of happiness rolling down my face.

The weekend went by quickly. Baby Axil and I met all of Ronny's family, and I was shown around town. It was a quaint little place with a population of around eight hundred people and a horse that lived on the main street, which gave new meaning to the term 'one-horse town'. The township closed for lunch each day for an hour from midday. It was a real country town in every sense of the word.

Before I knew it, Bobby had returned to take us home to Kempsey. I ran out when he pulled up, happy to see him, then heard Ronny call out to me. I returned inside and Ronny grabbed me softly by the shoulders. He pulled me close as he looked straight into my eyes and asked me ever so softly to stay. Although I was hesitant and my first thought was, *Go home, Ashlee*, there was something about the way he asked that convinced me to remain in town.

I walked outside to let Bobby know and Ronny came with me. I was a little shocked that he felt the need to accompany me. Maybe he could sense I was beginning to have second thoughts. As soon as I saw Bobby, I became emotional. I didn't know what to do. Bobby grabbed my arm and asked me if I was okay. I saw him glare at Ronny.

I answered, "I'm fine, but I'm just so confused."

Ronny then put his arm around my shoulder and assured me I would be okay. I apologised to Bobby for having come all the way to pick me up. I looked at him and said, "I think I'm going to stay another week or two."

Bobby frowned and looked surprised. He must have had an inkling of what was about to happen and feared for me as he asked, "Are you sure?"

Before I could answer, Ronny said, "Yeah, she's sure."

"Okay then," replied Bobby. "Call me if you need me, Ashlee." As he drove off I heard Ronny mumble something under his breath like, "You're lucky you fucked off." I then realise that I should have gotten into that car.

~

The first week was okay. Ronny's Aunty helped me with Axil. The following week his mum, sisters and brother visited every day.

On the second weekend, Ronny left to play football at Walgett while I stayed in Collarenebri. One of Ronny's cousins asked me to go uptown with him and I agreed. We walked up the main street, bought a bottle of Diet Coke at the local store and then sat in the park near the bowling club. The park had only a table and a slippery dip.

We sat down at the table and he began telling me stories about Ronny, and how he was actually in a relationship and living with another woman. I was absolutely and utterly shocked! I just couldn't believe what he was saying. He also warned me that the woman in question was going to confront me to let me know what had been going on.

When I returned to the house, I asked Ronny's sister whether any of the stories I had just heard were true. She acted like she didn't know what I was talking about. I went into the room and sat on the bed with an overwhelming feeling of anger and thought, *Yeah, just let her come and confront me*!

Ronny returned that afternoon on crutches because he had hurt his leg playing football. He told me it was just a little sprain. He asked if I wanted to go to the pub with him and said his cousin would mind Axil. I thought this would be my opportunity to get to the bottom of the story I had heard earlier that day, thinking that if his so-called 'girlfriend' was there, I could ask her in front of him. This way he couldn't lie and I would know the truth. I just had to keep my emotions in check; I was boiling on the inside.

I agreed and off we went. The pub was a five-minute walk from the house, so I wasn't too worried about leaving Axil as I was only going to be away for an hour.

It wasn't long before the other woman began letting me know what was going on.

She kept walking past him saying, "Hey, my man, what you doing?" She would then look at me and laugh.

I glanced at Ronny and asked, "Who's that?"

"No one, she's just being drunk and silly," he replied.

"That's not what I heard. I was told you are living with her."

Ronny looked at me and frowned, "No. Who told you that?"

"Don't you worry who told me," I replied. "If she walks past me again and says something, she's gonna get it. I don't give a fuck who she is."

Ronny just laughed it off. I told him I was going back to Axil and he said he would come too.

As we walked back I said to him, "I don't care what you do when I'm not here, but when I'm in town, can you just be with me?"

"You're my only woman, Ash, you got nothing to worry about," he said, and in my young, inexperienced mind, this was all I needed to hear.

After nearly two weeks in Collarenebri I began to feel homesick. I decided to call Bobby to see if he was coming out this way again and, as luck would have it, he was. I asked if he would please stop by and pick up Axil and me.

"Of course," he replied.

I was relieved as I had no idea how to get out of Collarenebri without a car.

I told Ronny that Bobby was coming to pick me up. He wasn't happy and stormed out of the house.At first I had no idea where he went. When I realised he had not taken the nappies off the line after I had asked him to, something inside me snapped.

I asked Ronny's cousin to watch Axil for a minute while I checked to see if Ronny was at the pub. I walked in and, sure enough, there he was dancing closely with his girlfriend. I saw red and ran straight at her, ready to hit her.

Ronny grabbed me before I could reach her and said, "Come on, let's go."

I tried to break free from his grip but couldn't. I told her to stay away from my man otherwise she was going to get it from me.

Ronny practically dragged me home, telling me how silly I was being and reassured me that I had nothing to worry about. I had barely settled down at the house when one of Ronny's cousins came around and asked him to go out drinking.

Ronny looked at me and said, "Babe, I'm just going up here for an hour or so ..." And off he went.

I wasn't too happy but, at the same time, I couldn't tell him not to go.

Later that night we got into a horrible fight, fuelled by my resentment of him not answering my letters. The rejection I felt came to a violent head. I lost control of my senses and, in a fit of rage, started to punch him.

He grabbed my hands and told me to wake up to myself but I just kept going. I remember hearing someone say, "Go in and stop that." I think it was his uncle.

I then heard his cousin say, "Let her go."

I was trying hard to hurt Ronny but he was too strong for me. I was screaming at him and swinging my arms around – I had truly lost all control. Ronny got up and left. I lay down and cried myself to sleep.

I was extremely embarrassed the next day, and sore. I felt as though a bus had hit me, even though Ronny didn't lay a hand on me. My ego was the most bruised of all. I felt so much shame from big noting myself in someone else's home and in a town I didn't come from. I was screaming on the inside, *Get me out of here*!

To say I was grateful to see Bobby when he arrived the next day would have been an understatement. I was packed and ready to leave with my son and my shame. As I was walking down the front steps, I apologised again for my terrible behaviour. Ronny barely looked at me, and who could blame him. He walked out to the car carrying Axil and kissed him as he put him in the capsule. I could see tears welling up in his eyes.

"I'm so sorry," I said, looking up at him. He put his arms around me and pulled me in towards him. I closed my eyes and nestled into his chest. He then whispered in my ear, "Will you stay?"

I shook my head, unable to look at him, and softly whispered, "No. I can't."

I pulled my body away from his, jumped into the car, and closed the door.

As we drove off, I didn't look back and I began to cry tears of shame, tears of hurt and regret but, most of all, tears of relief.

Four

The First Hit

I was so happy to be back in Kempsey. I couldn't thank Bobby enough for his generosity and understanding. He stayed overnight and headed off early the next morning. He said he would return in October for the Knockout that was being hosted in Macksville that year. I thanked him again and off he went.

I was so confused and caught up in my own mind after the Collarenebri trip that it took me a few days to get back to reality. Ronny began calling constantly. His phone calls were difficult. I had so many mixed emotions – the biggest one being guilt. Guilt for putting my hands on Ronny, guilt for not staying, guilt for feeling like I had trapped him somehow, guilt, guilt, guilt … I was filled with it.

Each time Ronny called, he would ask me when I was returning to Collarenebri. He really wanted Axil and me to come back, but I wasn't so sure.

I had been home for about two months when Ronny's cousin called me and told me she had organised a lift for us to travel to Collarenebri. They had a new teacher at the school, a Kempsey girl named Sara. Ronny's cousin had asked her to give us a lift on her return trip and Sara was more than happy to oblige.

I asked, "How will I get back?"

She explained she had organised for Ronny's sister to drive me to Moree to catch the train to Kempsey. I reluctantly agreed.

The trip was pleasant and I was really looking forward to seeing Ronny. We had been talking nearly every day on the phone and I felt we had really connected. Yet I wasn't sure how this was all going to turn out, and I really had no idea what I was doing or why. I just felt I needed to be with him. Before I knew it, I was back in Collywood, as I had come to call it.

We arrived late in the afternoon. The entire family was there to greet us. They were happy to see Axil and couldn't believe how big he had grown. I thanked Sara for giving us a lift. It had been a kind gesture.

The first night was magical. Ronny had set up the back room on the veranda for us and had even found a cot for Axil. It was our own little love nest. I actually began to feel loved during those first few days, and I couldn't believe how happy I felt. It was as if everything was just perfect – in my eyes anyway. Ronny and I spoke about our relationship and our future, and we both decided it was best if he came back to Kempsey with me.

Going back, however, didn't go as planned. Ronny's sister, who we were supposed to get a lift with to the train station, had run off with a married man and no one knew where she was. To make things worse, this man was married to her cousin. This was big news in a little town, and it was bad news for us as she was the only one who had a driver's licence.

I decided to call my family in Kempsey to see if anyone was willing to come all the way to Collarenebri to pick us up. It took a little persuasion, but they came through. I was so relieved when I saw my Aunties Angie and Tina, who had made the long trip. I was afraid I'd be stranded in Collarenebri with no way of getting home to Kempsey. They were grumbling and growling at how far it was and they were exhausted. They decided to stay the night.

A night turned into a couple of days and we decided to have a party. It was during this time that I started to notice how Ronny was paying a little too much attention to my Aunty Tina, and vice versa. I felt a pang of jealousy and uneasiness.

I thought I saw them sneaking glances at each other in a goo-goo-eyed kind of way, so I confronted Ronny. He told me to wake up to myself, and before long we were arguing.

A few people began mumbling, "I knew this would happen."

We ended up in a big fight. Ronny's brother Max stood up for me, and then the two of them began having a little push and shove. I threw a bottle at Ronny, which hit him on the left side of his forehead. When I saw blood drip from his head I became scared and ran back with Max to where Ronny and I had been sleeping.

We explained what had happened to Ronny's cousin, who was babysitting Axil. She was so good and told me to have a shower, then let me jump into her bed. After I woke up the next day, I walked into the room Ronny and I had been sharing to see if he had come home. He wasn't in bed. I then walked into the lounge room and found him asleep on the couch with a bandaid over his forehead. Apparently, he had needed medical attention.

I felt uncomfortable being around him, even more so when my Aunty Tina walked in. I'm not even sure she knew I was feeling this way. I didn't confront her about anything that had happened, or that I imagined had happened, the previous night. We decided to leave the next day, and I wasn't sure if Ronny was still coming back to Kempsey with me or not. We packed the car and got ready to head home. At the very last minute, Ronny decided to come with us. I think his Uncle Harry was the person who encouraged him as I heard him say, "I wouldn't let her or my son go without me."

Along the way, Tina decided to buy a carton of beer, and she and Ronny started drinking. This annoyed me as she kept turning around in the front seat to talk to Ronny who was in the back with Axil and me. It was like we were invisible, and my insecurities began to surface. Thank goodness for Aunty Angie. She was the driver and the only one out of the group of us who had any sense. I began wondering whether Ronny was coming to Kempsey for his son and me, or for Tina. I really thought I was losing my mind and became extremely paranoid whenever they were within sight of each other.

The first week was uneventful. We settled, somewhat, into each other's company and space. I do remember slyly watching Ronny every time my Aunty Tina was around. My jealousy took over my rational thinking.

We were into our third week of living together as a family in Kempsey when, one night, Ronny went off drinking. I had no idea where he was. I walked next door to my Aunty Angie's place and asked if she had seen him, but she hadn't. Just then Aunty Tina walked in. I almost expected Ronny to walk in behind her, such was my paranoia. I asked if she had seen him, and she said he was hanging around the top of Yarraville Street. There was a party going on at the top house. I thought to myself, *How do you know?*

I went looking for him and sure enough, I found him on Yarraville Street in a house known as the 'drinking house'. I walked to the front door and sang out to him. He came stumbling out, drunk. I asked him what he was doing. He replied in a half-smart way, "Drinking," as if I couldn't tell.

"Well, you best come home with me now," I said.

He nodded in a half-hearted way. We started walking towards home when he began to carry on about not being able to do what he wanted and asked me why he couldn't keep drinking.

He accused me of being jealous, and then he whacked me with the back of his hand straight across the left side of my face. There was so much force behind the blow that I thought he had broken my cheekbone. My head felt like it had spun around and I could feel my face immediately begin to swell. I screamed and swung back trying to hit him but missed.

I started running down the road towards home, crying, while he took off in the opposite direction. My face was pounding and I couldn't see out of my left eye from the swelling. Everything was blurry, but somehow I managed to run to Nan's house and stumbled through the door.

Aunty Tina started to blame me as soon as she saw me. "Well, you went looking for him," she said.

I didn't reply but I remember thinking that she was the one who had told me where he was. I began wondering again how exactly she knew where he was. Nan advised me to call the police, but I didn't take her advice. I didn't know what to do, what to feel or how to act, and so I cried and did nothing.

Ronny, on the other hand, decided to steal a car and break into the local golf club.

I was sitting on the back porch with Aunty Angie, recovering from that first hit with tears rolling down my swollen face, when I heard a car roaring down the hill at full speed towards Middleton Street.

Angie and I said in unison, "Shit, who's that?" We ran out the front to investigate.

It was Ronny. He saw us and began spinning the car around, doing doughnuts outside Nan's place. I thought, *What an idiot!* That day was filled with warning signs for me to stay away from Ronny, but I chose to ignore them.

Later that night, Ronny came home. He was now hiding from the police. He walked into our room, where our son was asleep in his crib. I had just had a shower and was sitting on the end of my bed feeling distraught and rubbing Vicks onto my swollen face to help bring out the bruise so it would heal faster.

Ronny walked into the room and froze when he saw the damage he had done to my face. He closed the door behind him. My heart skipped a beat when I saw his demeanour change. It was as if he was shocked to see my battered face. He dropped to his knees, held me tight around my hips, put his head in my lap and began to cry. He said how sorry he was and how much he loved Axil and me. I started to weep alongside him. My heart swelled with emotion as I softly kissed the top of his head.

In that second, all seemed to be forgiven. He stood up, took me into his strong arms and told me he loved me. Even though he still reeked of alcohol, I didn't care. All that mattered was that he loved me.

He gently kissed my puffed-up face and then my mouth, like he'd never kissed me before. He was gentle, passionate and loving. It was like I was floating in space surrounded by stars. He had my mind, body and soul. I was consumed by what I thought was love and so my addiction to him intensified.

~

The next few months went by, and although I was still a little concerned about the goings on between Ronny and Tina, I fell deeper and deeper in love with him.

One Friday night Ronny drove to Port Macquarie with my aunties. Four of them went with him – Tina, Claudia, Cynthia and Angie. I didn't mind; he was with my family after all.

On their return at around 3am, I heard them traipse into the house and waited for Ronny to come into our bedroom. He didn't. I got up and walked out into the kitchen, and spotted Angie on the back veranda having a smoke. I asked her where Ronny was. She said they couldn't wake him up so they had left him in the car. I walked out to the car.

It was dark and a little chilly, and the car windows were foggy, which I thought was strange. I opened the door and my heart stopped. There in the back seat was Tina with her head resting on Ronny's shoulder. I tried waking him but he wouldn't budge, so I decided to leave him there. A little while later he wandered into the bedroom and I pretended to be asleep. I decided not to say anything. I chose to wait until the morning when he was sober.

The next day I confronted Ronny and asked him why on earth he would he stay in the car with Tina. I told him I had tried to wake him and then accused him of pretending to be asleep. We had a few more harsh words, and he stormed off.

Tina, all fresh from a shower, came walking into the kitchen and said, "He had a good night, you know." She had a little smirk on her face when she said it.

I thought to myself, *I'm sure he did*. I was convinced something was going on but still refused to confront her about it.

A few days passed and I was in the backyard hanging out the washing, when a girl named Mary walked past and sang out to me. I walked over to the back fence.

"I seen Tina and Ronny rolling around over the park last night," she said bluntly.

"What?" I replied. "Doing what?"

"Rolling around, you know," she said, rolling her eyes, "I thought you should know."

I thanked her and continued to peg the clothes thinking, *This can't be true!*

Not long afterwards, I spoke to my Aunty Mimi about the situation. Her advice was that if it was true I should leave Ronny, but I didn't want to do that. I decided to confront them instead.

Later that afternoon when it was just the three of us in the house, I built up the courage to speak my mind. Aunty Tina was sitting out the back having a smoke. I went out to join her. I knew Ronny would follow me, as I had noticed he didn't like us being alone together.

He walked out and sat down. I stood up and started firing questions at them. My heart was pounding, adrenaline rushing, and my mouth wouldn't stop!

"So what the fuck is going on between you two, hey?

"What happened in the car last night?

"Why the fuck did you pretend to be asleep?

"What do you want from him, Tina?

"Did you come over here for her, Ronny? Did ya?"

Neither of them said a word. I screamed, "Answer me! What's wrong with you two?"

Ronny got up, grabbed my arm and simply said, "Nothing's going on. I'm here for you and Axil. You're my woman."

And that was that.

Ronny had been in Kempsey for two months. It was now mid September 1992. One night he and I went up to my Uncle Floyd and his partner Lucy's place. Ronny was drinking again. Floyd and Lucy went to sleep when Ronny began talking to me about my confrontation with him and Tina. He called me sick and jealous, and began working himself up. Then he grabbed me and plonked me down on a chair beside him. He suddenly punched me in the arm and said, "That's for being a bitch."

He then punched me again and said, "That's for believing lies."

And on it went, ending with, "That's because I love you."

I just sat there, too scared to move. He let go of my arm and I got up and ran around the table. He started to chase me and I screamed, "Leave me alone!"

My Uncle Floyd appeared and growled, "You two better stop it! There are kids asleep here. Get to bed." Ronny then held my arm and led me into the room. We lay down, Ronny cuddled up to me, trapping me with his arm, and we fell asleep.

The next day my arm was black, blue and purple from shoulder to elbow. It was so swollen and sore that I couldn't even lift my baby. I showed my Aunty Angie who gasped and said, "Ash, you gotta do something. Why don't you go down to your Mum in Sydney?"

I took her advice, and she drove me to Port Macquarie so I could sneak away quickly. That night I left for Sydney with my son.

Mum welcomed Axil and me with open arms. She asked where Ronny was. I lied and told her everything was okay, that he was doing a course so he would be down in a few days, and that I just wanted her to spend some time with her grandson. I'm not sure if she believed me, but she never questioned me.

Ronny began calling me at my mother's place, crying about me leaving him in Kempsey on his own, and wondering what he was supposed to do.

A week later, he was on a train to collect me.

Five

Betrayal

You can imagine my surprise when both Ronny and Tina turned up at Mum's place together. They just waltzed into the house without a care in the world.

"When did you get here?" I asked Tina suspiciously.

"I came down with Ronny on the train," she replied matter-of-factly.

I almost choked on her smugness. Her reply immediately infuriated me, and my mind began spinning with the implications of what she actually meant. I felt like punching her in the mouth. I looked at her and thought, *You're not taking my man.*

Soon after, Ronny and I disappeared into the bedroom. We were completely in the moment and behaved as if nothing negative had happened between us in the past. At least, that was my way of dealing with it – ignore the red flags and inhabit the world of denial. We began giggling and kissing.

Tina walked past the door, which was ajar, and said in disgust, "You two make me sick."

I turned my attention to her and and asked with satisfaction, "Why's that?"

She stormed off. I couldn't help but laugh internally as though I had the upper hand. I didn't care what she thought because I had my man back.

The next day, Ronny, Axil, Tina and I went to visit our cousin Macy who lived on the Block in Eveleigh Street, Redfern. Aside from being a place for Aboriginal people to live and gather, the Block was notorious in the media for drugs and violence. But it felt like home to me. I had lots of family and friends who lived on the Block and I loved going there because it represented a sense of community.

We reached Macy's place. She lived at the end of Eveleigh Street in a townhouse that had a little brick fence and a big tree out the front, so you could sit in the shade and watch the goings on. On that particular occasion, we just hung out in the lounge room, drinking tea and gossiping.

Tina asked Macy if she could ring Nan on her landline. Macy agreed, so she picked up the phone and called Nan. As Tina began talking to Nan she became upset, passed me the phone and said, "Mum wants to talk to you."

Tina seemed nervous and became more agitated, so I asked if she was okay. She just handed me the receiver.

I said, "Hello Nan, what's happening?"

Nan asked me how Axil and I were. There was a little bit of small talk, then she told me she was concerned about me, and mentioned that she thought there was something going on with Tina and Ronny.

Her exact words were, "Something's not right, they're up to no good."

I automatically turned to look at Tina, who was now extremely distressed. She met my gaze and screamed out, "Don't believe her! It's just yarns!"

I was shocked and confused at Tina's outburst. I told Nan I loved her and ended the conversation, before turning to look Tina right in the eyes. For the first time I asked her directly, "Are you sleeping with Ronny?"

"No! It's nothing like that!" she said and burst out crying. I didn't believe her.

I continued to stare at her, as if I could somehow read her mind and see what she was thinking, when suddenly I felt a wave of disappointment wash over me. I turned and walked away. I grabbed Axil, strapped him into the pram, strode out the front door, and started walking up Eveleigh Street with tears stinging my eyes. I was determined not to show her my pain.

I loved Tina like a sister and we were always together, so I just couldn't comprehend what Nan had told me. All I knew was that Nan wouldn't lie. I felt betrayed and confused. Just then I heard footsteps behind me. It was Ronny. He grabbed my arm, spun me around and asked, "What's going on?"

"You tell me," I replied.

He looked at me, his eyes searching mine for clues, and said, "What happened, babe?"

I repeated to him what Nan had just told me.

He looked at me, unsure what to say.

"Is it true? Are you and Tina getting it on?" I asked.

He didn't deny it, nor did he admit it. His face became blank. He was hard to read.

Then he responded, "Did you ask Tina?"

I told him I had, and he wanted to know what she had said. Without thinking, I told him Tina had denied it. Then he looked me right in the eye and said, "That's right, nothing's going on."

He then grabbed the pram out of my hands and said, "Come on, let's go." We walked down to Mum's place barely saying a word to each other.

Once I settled down and reflected on the day, I couldn't help but wonder what Ronny might have said if I had pretended that Tina had admitted it. Would he have left me for her? Would he? Maybe … I felt a shiver down my spine at the thought of having to see them together and shook my head to get the image from my mind. I guess I'll never know.

The next few days were uneventful. Ronny decided that because we were in Sydney, we should attend the Knockout. Apparently he was a deadly football player and someone would give him a run. That year, the event was being held in Blacktown.

The Knockout began in 1970, with only a handful of teams. Now it is played over three full days across the October Labour Day long weekend in New South Wales, attracting over sixty of the hardest and fastest rugby league teams you will ever see. The players shed blood, sweat and tears until there is only one team left standing. It is known to many as a modern-day corroboree and a meeting place for family and friends. It's one of the biggest annual gatherings of Aboriginal people in Australia – players come from everywhere.

It was a warm, sunny day in early October, and Ronny was hurrying me along to get Axil and myself ready to catch the train to Blacktown. I didn't understand his enthusiasm. It was the most excited I had ever seen him outside of when he was revving himself up to drink.

Off we went – our 'happy' little family. When we reached our destination, I immediately started looking for all my Aunties. Cynthia, Halle and Tina were already there, so I sat down with them. We began talking, laughing and joking around while all taking turns at holding and playing with Axil. I must have been having too much fun because suddenly – from behind, and seemingly out of nowhere – Ronny grabbed my hair, twisted it in his hand, pulled my head back and said, "Do you want a hiding?"

I felt so embarrassed. My eyes began to well up. I fought the tears and whispered, "No, let me go. What's wrong with you?"

"Fuck off, Ronny! Let her go and leave her alone!" demanded Cynthia.

He eventually pulled his hand away. He had a little smirk on his face. This was the first time he displayed this behaviour in public, and it wouldn't be the last. I barely saw him for the remainder of the day. He flitted back and forth, and later in the afternoon, as I prepared to get a lift back to Mum's place, he ran up to me all excited and happy. I was puzzled, and then he said, "Hey Ash, can you give me fifty dollars?"

"What for?" I asked.

"I'm going to have a few beers with the boys," he replied.

"Okay," I said as I handed over the cash. "How are you getting home?"

"With my mates. See you later," he said. There was no kiss, no nothing. Off he ran in his happy little mood, with my money, and he didn't make it home that night.

I decided not to go to the footy the next day. Instead, I spent the day with Mum. It was nice, although Ronny wasn't far from my mind. Later that afternoon my aunties came down to visit and asked me if I wanted to go out with them. I told them I didn't have a babysitter. Although Mum was helpful with material things and had an abundance of love for her grandson, she refused to change a nappy or get up to feed him. Thankfully, my sister Lara said she would mind him and I told her I wouldn't be out late.

Off we went to the Blacktown RSL Club. It was pumping. There were

Blackfullas from all over New South Wales. Tina, Halle, Cynthia and I were grooving on the dance floor, showing all the other girls how deadly Kempsey girls could dance. We were having a ball, when suddenly Ronny appeared.

Fuck, I thought, *I hope he doesn't start on me*. Thankfully, he didn't. He just said, "I'll catch up with you later," and vanished into the crowd. I thought to myself, *That's strange. I wonder what's going on with him*. In that moment, I really didn't care as I was having too much fun with my family. From the corner of my eye, I saw him checking on me a few more times during the night. Each time I saw him, I stopped laughing and dancing so much, pretending that I wasn't having as much fun as I was.

Later that night, as my aunties and I were heading home, I saw Ronny jump into a car with a girl named Leah. She was very attractive and a few years older than me. Her hair went all the way down past her bum. I thought she was beautiful. Before I could sing out to Ronny, the car took off. I didn't see Ronny again until Monday night. He came to Mum's place all sad and sorry. I ignored him until I saw a red-purple mark on his neck.

"What the fuck is that?" I demanded, pointing to his neck.

"What?" he replied, as he tried to cover it up with his hand.

"Is that a love bite?" I asked.

He looked at me blankly and just shook his head. I was furious and asked again, "Who gave you that love bite, you dirty cheating dog?" Then I shouted, "Fuck off!"

I was enraged and couldn't believe he would do such a thing to me – I thought he loved me.

"Don't come bringing your dirty scales home to me and my son," I continued and stormed out into the backyard. I lit a smoke and just sat thinking, *What a fucking dead cunt.*

He followed me out, came up to me and said, "I don't know what you're going on about. You're the one who put it on my neck."

I looked up and said, "Get fucked, dickhead! I never sucked anything of yours over the weekend!"

I couldn't believe how brave I felt, swearing at him and challenging him. It felt good. For the first time, I felt like I had a little bit of power over him. He then made up some nonsense yarn and said that when he came over to talk to me, I had given him a kiss and a cuddle and sucked on his neck. His statement confused me and I started to question myself, thinking, *Had I? I was a little bit charged up, so maybe I did?* I couldn't remember. I looked at him, puzzled.

He suddenly grabbed me and said, "Why would I cheat on you? I have everything I want right here."

He pulled me close, kissed me passionately and assured me I had nothing to worry about. And just like that, I convinced myself that I must have given him the love bite after all?

Six

Out of the Fire into the Flames

Two days later we headed back to Kempsey. The police had been to Nan's place looking for Ronny regarding a reckless driving incident, and the break and enter of the golf club. Ronny became wary of every knock on the door. A few days later the police charged him with stealing a car and the break and enter, and he was to appear at Kempsey Court House in six weeks.

He seemed to settle down a bit after this. He became attentive and actively involved in our day-to-day living, which made me fall even more deeply in love with him. Life was good. He even watched Axil one night so I could go and see Yothu Yindi when they played a concert at the local school. I actually felt happy.

One night about a week later, we woke to the sounds of screaming, "Get out! Get out! The house is on fire!"

Ronny immediately jumped up, opened the door and saw Aunty Cynthia crawling on her hands and knees with her son Eli, Aunty Angie's daughter Brittney and Aunty Mimi's son Cayne behind her. She said, "Stay down and move slow." He quickly closed the door.

"Get up, babe!" he screamed.

I jumped up. He opened the window, knocked the screen out of it and said, "You have to jump."

"No way," I said. "What about Axil?"

"You have to," he pleaded. "You jump out first then I'll pass Axil down to you. Now hurry up!"

I climbed up onto the windowsill and looked out. The drop was four metres and I was petrified. Ronny kept screaming behind me, "JUMP! JUMP! JUMP!"

I turned to look at him. Before I knew it, he picked me up and threw me out the window. As I fell, I scraped the entire inside of my arms. I hit the ground, dazed, trying to get up.

He grabbed Axil and shouted down, "Ashlee, get a fucking grip. Stand still and catch our son."

Then, as gently as possible, he dropped Axil down to me. I backed away and then Ronny jumped. Just as he hit the ground, the roof caved in and we all ran to the back fence. I believe he saved our livesthat day. He was now a hero. As a result, my love and addiction to him grew deeper.

As we huddled in the back, screaming and talking all at once, I asked Cynthia, "How did you know the house was on fire?" She explained how the milkman had been banging on the door screaming at everyone to get out and shouting that the house was on fire. It was the milkman who saved us. Everyone made it out safely. Sally and Graham, our neighbours who lived behind us, came over to check on us. One of Sally's daughters gave me a nappy for Axil, who by this time was crying for his morning feed and a bottle. Thankfully, Lucy had made a fresh bottle for her son and she gave it to Axil. We were safe and that was all that mattered.

The fire brigade was quick to put the fire out. We weren't allowed inside. Ronny, however, jumped through the window to grab my purse, as well as some nappies and clothes for Axil.

We made it into the local paper. Pop was interviewed and photographed. He was concerned about us, especially the little ones. There was an investigation and the fire brigade concluded the fire was caused by an electrical fault in the lounge room.

Nan flew into action, and the community came together to help us out with clothes and food. Nan's niece Nelly, who worked for the local council, was a really big help to the family during this difficult time.

Nan was rehoused in North Street. I didn't want to stay there because it would be too crowded with Aunty Mimi, her sons Cayne and Brock, her partner Frank and Uncle Matt, so I asked Cynthia and Dan if Ronny,

Axil and I could stay with her at Little Rudder Street. Thankfully, she agreed and told us we could live downstairs. Cynthia lived in a three-storey terrace house. Downstairs was one big open-plan room. A staircase led to the second level, which contained the lounge room, one bedroom and the bathroom with a separate toilet. Another smaller set of stairs led to the third level where there was a second bedroom, kitchen, dining room and laundry – and a door, which led outside to the backyard. We settled in and our routine continued.

Ronny's court day arrived quickly. He contemplated not going, fearing he would be sent to jail. I convinced him it would be better for all of us if he went, that if he didn't he would only be making it worse. He eventually agreed with me.

We attended court as scheduled. I was scared and so was Ronny. It was the first time in my life I had ever entered a courtroom. I think I was more nervous than he was. The hearing went well – much better than Ronny's solicitor had led us to believe. The judge sentenced Ronny to a one-year good behaviour bond, and warned him that if he so much as jaywalked, he would be sent straight to jail. We were all relieved, so much so that when Ronny suggested he needed a drink, I agreed.

Cynthia agreed to watch Axil, and Dan warned us that if we came home fighting we would have to deal with him – which was rather ironic because he and Cynthia fought regularly.

We went out and everyone was having a great time. I met up with a few of my friends, and after the club closed we decided to party on the riverbank. It was the most fun I had had in a long time, but it didn't last.

Ronny started to argue with me over absolutely nothing, saying things like, "Gee you're having fun. Who are you looking at?" and so on.

I asked him, "What's wrong with you?"

He just gave me a filthy look and then started to push me around. He had a habit of grabbing me on the back of my neck and twisting my hair in his hand. Sometimes he would lift me off the ground by my hair and neck.

I begged him, "No please don't, Ronny, we're having such a good time."

His answer was to throw me to the ground. I fell onto my left side and began sliding down an embankment on my backside as if I was on a slippery dip. He then ran down and grabbed me by the hair before punching me in the face. I looked up at him in pure terror and put my hands up instinctively to protect my face as my body slumped. I started shaking my head, begging him, "Ronny, please don't."

He raised his right hand into a fist above his shoulder ready to hit me again, when he suddenly changed his mind. Instead, he grabbed my hair, jerked my head back, pushed me aside and ordered me to, "Get the fuck home."

I took off across the traffic bridge and kept running all the way back to Cynthia's place.

I immediately ran up to the bathroom to look at my face in the mirror. There was only a slight welt so I thought to myself, *Thank goodness. I can cover that up easily*.

I jumped into the shower and as the water hit my body, I flinched. *Fuck*, I thought, as tears stung my eyes. I had forgotten that I had fallen, and looked down to notice that the left side of my body had been grazed. I jumped out, dried myself carefully, rubbed some pawpaw ointment on my side, and put my PJs on. I then grabbed Axil from Cynthia's room and cuddled up to him before drifting off to sleep.

Ronny didn't come home that night. I was relieved. I didn't want my family to know he had hit me again. The next day, I checked myself in the mirror again. My face was okay – there was only a little swelling, which was hardly noticeable. My side, however, was red and sore. I must have fallen on rocks or gravel. I cleaned myself up, applied more pawpaw ointment and then walked with Axil to South Kempsey to visit Uncle Floyd and Lucy. Lucy took one look at my face and knew what had happened. I confided in Lucy about my situation because I knew she would understand me. I had witnessed my uncle hit her on a few occasions, so I knew I was safe with her. It turned out Floyd had hit her on the previous night too.

Here we were: two young mothers, both in tears and covered with bruises, trying to help each other out the best way we knew how. I found a new love and respect for Lucy that morning and vowed to myself that no matter what, I would always have her back, just as she had mine. She told me to stay for the night.

"I'll make us some dinner. You go and bath Axil," she said.

I was putting Axil into the bathe when suddenly Ronny walked into the bathroom. My heart stopped. He pulled the door closed behind him, looked at me, and asked if I was okay.

I was shaking and couldn't fathom how to answer. I could see he was becoming frustrated and angry with me. I was frozen and had never felt such fear in my life, until I heard Mum's voice sing out. I nearly collapsed with relief. I hadn't known that she was coming to Kempsey.

"Go out and see her," said Ronny calmly. "I'll finish bathing Axil."

I trembled as I walked out into the lounge room and managed to give her a smile, all the while trying to hide the right side of my swollen face with my hair.

I asked her, "What are you doing here?"

"I decided to come up for Christmas," she replied. "Where's Axil?"

"In the bathtub," I replied as she followed me into the bathroom.

She gave Axil a big kiss, then glared at Ronny and said in the calmest voice, "If my grandson wasn't in here I'd smash your head into that bathtub! You lay one hand on my daughter again and you'll have me to deal with."

I just stood there with my eyes wide open, terrified of Ronny's response.

Ronny smirked and nodded his head once. I didn't know where to look or what to do, so I just stood there. Mum walked out and said to me, "I'll deal with you later," and left. I was now even more nervous and anxious. My life had turned into a living hell, but over the next couple of days everything seemed to settle down again.

Christmas came before we knew it. We all gathered at the North Street house. Ronny, Floyd and Pop were having a beer outside while watching Axil, who was crawling around everywhere. I was watching as he splashed around in his new pool. It was just a little plastic blow-up pool, but he seemed to love it. I could see Ronny was uncomfortable with Mum being around. Then Mum went up to talk to him and ended up giving him a cuddle. I was confused.

I asked her later, "What was that about?"

"I was just sitting here watching him," she replied, "and he looked sad, so I thought to myself I may as well make amends with him because he isn't worth losing my daughter over."

And that was that.

From that day on, Mum became Ronny's biggest advocate – not straight away, but over the years. I often had extreme feelings of resentment over this.

Ronny's behaviour improved for a while ... and I mean only for a while. New Year's Eve came and went with no real dramas, and then it was Ronny's birthday on 6 January. He, of course, wanted to go out, but I didn't want to accompany him so I went to bingo with my family while he went out with Floyd.

On my return home, my Aunty Angie's partner Bryce, who was looking after his daughter Brittney and Axil at Cynthia's place, said, "Ash, you're never going to believe what I just saw ..."

"What?" I asked.

He proceeded to explain how he had seen Ronny rolling around, kissing a girl named Deena under the streetlight across the road just two metres away from where we were staying.

"Who and what?" I asked.

"You know Deena, the one who stays down the end flat," he explained.

I vaguely recalled her and nodded. "Where are they now?" I asked.

"I don't know. They might be in the flat," he replied.

I took a deep breath, went upstairs, had a shower and sobbed. I couldn't believe he had done this to me again.

"We've been going so good ... boo hooo hooo!" I wept.

After a cry, I dressed myself and decided to look for him. As I stepped out onto the street, I spotted him walking towards me. Something snapped in me and I started.

"What the fuck were you doing with Deena under the streetlight, ya dirty dog? You're nothing but a slut with balls! You make me sick! I hope your cock drops off!" I screamed.

As usual, he went into a state of complete denial.

"Who? What the fuck are you talking about?" he spat out while smirking.

I was thinking, *What a fucking DOG! I hate your guts. Stay the fuck away from my son and me, you piece of shit!* I then picked up a stick and ran at him.

He took off up the road and I chased after him, screaming, "I'll kill you, ya cunt." And then he was gone. I turned around still carrying my stick. I could see people looking at me from the front flat as I screamed to Deena, who was inside, "You can have him, ya slut!"

I was half hoping she would come out so I could hit her with the stick, which I more than likely would have done.

The next day as I was walking along the traffic bridge coming into town, I crossed the road and saw Ronny sitting with my Uncle Floyd at the pub. He was laughing and *cooeeing*. I looked to see who he was calling out to because it certainly wasn't me. It wasn't me, it was Deena. He suddenly saw me, and they took off in the opposite direction. My uncle looked at me, smiled and waved, completely oblivious to the goings on. I thought, *Fuck them all!* And just kept walking.

Then Ronny came up behind me.

"You'd better fuck off, Ronny, or I'm going to call the police," I said. The threat seemed to work, so I went about my business and then walked home. Later that afternoon, Ronny walked into Cynthia's place.

"You'd better fuck off, mate," I said.

"I'm hungry," he replied.

"Yeah, well go ask Deena for a feed. Fuck off down there."

"I just want a sandwich," he went on.

"You touch one slice of bread and I'm calling the police. Now fuck off out of this house!"

He threw his head back and laughed. I picked up the phone and I called the police.

They answered, "Emergency. Who are you after? Fire, ambulance or police?"

I answered, "Police please."

The operator connected me to the police, and I asked the person on the other end of the line if they could come out to remove my partner who was being aggressive. Ronny immediately took off up the road, cursing and carrying on. I hung up the phone and didn't see or hear from him for two days. He called me on his payday and asked me to meet him. I agreed, convincing myself I needed money.

As soon as I saw him, I began to cry. I don't even know why. He grabbed me and held me close and said, "Everything's going to be okay, Ash."

I don't know why I believed him, but I did.

I wasn't sure if Ronny was allowed back at Cynthia's place, so I asked her. She told me he was no longer welcome. He ended up renting a motel room for the night and asked me to stay with him so we could figure things out, and I did.

Ronny was putting Axil to sleep when he turned to me and said, "Ash, you know I love you hey, and there's nothing I wouldn't do for you and our son."

I looked at him and felt my heart aching. I then began questioning him. "Then why did you go with Deena?"

"I didn't," he protested. "Are you going to believe Bryce over me? I'll punch the lying cunt in the face. Bryce's nothing but a lying fuck!"

I didn't remember telling him Bryce had told me, so I said quietly, "It's okay, just tell me the truth."

He looked me in the eye and said, "I swear to you, Ashlee, I never slept with her. You're my woman and I love you."

I started to cry and told him I couldn't take him being with anyone else – that it would kill me. He told me I had nothing to worry about, then took me into his strong arms and kissed me. I overdosed on my addiction that night to numb the pain.

The next day Ronny decided that the best thing for him to do was to go to Taree with my Uncle Matt. He said this was a good idea because I had called the police on him and he believed they would now want to arrest him. I agreed he should leave, and actually felt guilty for my actions.

A few days later I ran into one of my good friends, who had just returned from Taree. She told me she had heard rumours that Ronny was in town, hooking up with another girl and that they had been caught having sex, or rolling around, under the streetlight in the park. I thought to myself, *Get fucked! Really? What's this business with streetlights?*

This information tipped me over the edge, and I decided to call the police and follow through with charging Ronny with assaulting me. I ended up applying for my very first apprehended violence order (AVO).

An AVO protects victims of domestic violence who are fearful of future violence or have had threats to their safety. They are sometimes called restraining orders or protection orders.

As ashamed as I am to admit it, I will say this: I reported Ronny to the police out of pure spite for him cheating on me. It wasn't so much for the beatings, but the cheating. By doing what I did and thinking in this way, I realise in hindsight that I still had a long way to go before I could completely acknowledge the truth about what was happening to me and the truth about what I had become.

Seven
Jail Wife

A few days later, the police picked up Ronny in Taree.

He made his one phone call to me, screaming down the line, "You put an AVO out on me didn't you, ya slut ... didn't YOU! You better watch out!" Before he could say any more I hung up the phone.

The next day he was transferred to Kempsey Police Station. He called me again – this time begging me to visit him. I ran over to Kempsey Police Station as quickly as I could. I asked the police if I could reverse the AVO and drop the charges. They seemed frustrated with me, and tried to explain how important it was that I went through with the AVO. I didn't want to hear what they were saying – I just wanted to drop everything. They advised me I couldn't and I didn't understand why. My heart sank. I couldn't believe what I had done and was consumed with guilt.

I was allowed to visit Ronny in the cells. As soon as I laid eyes on him, I begged him for forgiveness. I couldn't comprehend what I had done. This was my fault. My man, my love, my baby's daddy was going to jail because of me – because of my jealous ways. I was a bad person, a terrible woman and a horrible mother who deliberately sent her baby's father away. Who would do that? Me. I felt like the lowest of the low. The guilt and the shame were almost unbearable and I could barely hold it together, but I had to be strong for my son and my man. I vowed in that moment that I would support Ronny in every way that was needed. I would be the best jail wife ever!

Ronny looked at me and cried, "I'm sorry, babe, sorry for all the things I've done."

"No, it's not your fault. I'm sorry," I replied. "I tried to take the AVO off. I'm so sorry. I love you, Ronny."

We both held each other through the bars and cried.

The next day he had to go to court. I borrowed Nan's car to drive to the courthouse. They let me visit him again to bring him his court clothes and some smokes. He looked so handsome in his crisp white shirt and black trousers. I thought, *I'm so lucky he chose me.*

When it was his turn to appear, he stood up and listened as the judge read out his charges. There were additional charges of resisting arrest in Taree and stealing from a person. I looked at him and frowned and – for a fleeting moment – I realised it wasn't entirely my fault. My attention quickly returned to Ronny. The judge gave him leniency because he had a partner and a baby. Instead of eighteen months, he only had to do six. I was relieved for a split second, and then panic overtook me and I crumbled into a heap. The guilt completely enveloped me. If I had not filed the AVO against him, none of this would have happened. How was I going to cope without Ronny for a full six months? My lover, my man, my drug. The police took him back to the cells and let me see him one more time.

"Ashlee, I love you. Will you wait for me?" he asked.

"Of course," I replied, as I grabbed his hands through the cell bars and entwined our fingers.

He told me they were going to take him to the Grafton jail at 7am the next morning. I kissed him goodbye through the bars and told him I would see him soon.

The next morning, I drove to the police station at 6.30am. I sat in the car barely blinking as I watched the station, afraid I might miss seeing the police bring him out. The prison van pulled up and I watched intently as they put Ronny inside along with a few other men. My heart ached as I began to cry uncontrollably. The van drove off and I followed it all the way down the highway, crying and beeping the car horn, hoping he would hear me and know I loved him. I pulled over to the side of the road just before Frederickton and began to weep, longing for my man, who I had just had incarcerated.

The first time I visited Ronny in jail was scary. It was the following weekend and I was not sure what to expect. I caught the morning train to Grafton, and thankfully Axil was a good traveller. In fact, he was a good baby all the time. He ate and then slept for four hours, had a little play, ate again, then slept for another four hours. He was a happy baby too, and he filled my life with more love than I ever thought possible. I loved that little boy, and it pains me to remember how much my actions and choices would affect him in the future.

The train ride was nice. I had a lot of time to think about what a bad person I was for putting my baby's daddy in jail. After a while I pushed the thought out of my mind and focused instead on the love I had for Ronny, and how good it would feel to hold him in my arms again.

We arrived in Grafton in the late afternoon. It was jacaranda season and the roads and pathways were lined with beautiful trees in full bloom with deep lilac-purple flowers. I had arranged to stay at a halfway house for women who were visiting their husbands, partners and boyfriends in jail. When I arrived, I was welcomed, given a print-out of the rules and regulations, a tour, and then shown to my room. It was a simple room with a double bed and a cupboard – and not much else. *It'll do*, I said to myself.

I gave Axil a bath and a feed, then put him on a blanket on the floor so he could play for a while. I organised our clothes for our visit, making sure I had Ronny's jocks and socks, money for drinks, chips and lollies, and fifty dollars to put into his account. Everything was ready, so we settled in for the night. I fell into a light sleep, holding onto Axil tightly. I was excited to see Ronny, but also scared to be sleeping in an unfamiliar place.

The next day we woke up and left early as visiting hours were from nine to three and I wanted to be the first one there. When I arrived, I was stunned to see a long line in front of me. I thought I was early, but so did all the other women standing in the queue holding babies in their arms and swapping notes on why their menfolk had been incarcerated. I was overwhelmed. I looked around and thought, *I'm not like any of these women. They seem so desperate*. The truth was – when I finally admitted it – I WAS just like every other woman in that line. We were all the same.

Eventually, it was my turn and I was shocked to discover that visits only lasted for two hours.

"Two hours?" I exclaimed to the female corrections officer behind the counter, who seemed friendly enough.

"But I've travelled all the way from Kempsey! It took me three hours to get here."

"Sorry to burst your bubble, but most of these women have travelled a whole day to get here," she replied in a matter-of-fact, no-nonsense tone.

I handed her my green visitor's form. I had filled it out with information such as my name, address, relationship to the inmate and their 'min number' (which is their prison ID number). This would become Ronny's jail number for the rest of his life. I still know the number today.

Finally, my name was called. I had to walk through a metal detector with Axil in my arms and was asked to take off all my jewellery. We then proceeded through the first gate, paused in a cell for a minute while the next gate opened, and then we were led through a large door. We walked down a corridor to a desk where we handed our green form over to the officers. After that, we were led into the visiting room.

I searched the room for Ronny and saw him smiling and waving at me. He stood up, dressed in big white overalls, and I walked over to him with tears in my eyes. He put his arms around both Axil and me and then kissed me. I felt woozy and in love. He took our son, put him on his knee and started kissing him and telling him how much he missed him. We then started talking, small talk really, like, "How you are going? What have you been doing? Have you been going out?"

I answered, "Good, not much," and a resounding, "No way would I go out while you're in here!"

I asked him how he was doing. "Is it okay? Is it scary? Is it safe?"

He laughed and assured me it was all good, and then started to cry. I thought, *What the fuck?* And I asked again, "Are you okay?" He shook his head.

I looked around to see if anyone was watching him, but what I saw was a repeat of the same scenario at every visitor's station. All the men in white overalls zipped up at the back with a padlock, sat across from their wives, girlfriends and children, heads bent as though weeping. I was shocked and didn't quite know how to react. We weren't allowed to touch the prisoners – our loved ones – intimately. I put my hands on his knees, looked him straight in the eye and reassured him, "It's going to be okay, babe, we'll get through this."

He looked at me with his dark brown eyes and told me he loved me, and that he was sorry for all he had done. He then went on to give me a few rules to live by:

I was not to go out – he had better not hear I had been with another man.

I was to visit him at least every second weekend.

I had to be at home to answer his phone calls.

I had to send him money for 'buy up' every week.

I agreed wholeheartedly and told him I would never go with another man, and I meant it. I had already made the decision to be the best jail wife ever, so his rules were ones that would be easy to live by.

Our visit went by exceptionally fast. An officer came over and told Ronny it was time to wrap up. Ronny then stood up and put his hand around my shoulder, and we walked to the exit door together. In my mind there was nobody else in the room. I put Axil on my hip so I could feel Ronny's body pressed against mine – it was the most delirious embrace I had ever felt. I then tilted my head back to receive his kiss and thought, *God, I love this man*. We kissed again and said goodbye.

A guard escorted Ronny from the table. I glanced over at him and said, "I love you Ronny." I meant it with every part of my being.

"I love you too," he replied. "Take care of my son."

Axil and I left and walked back to the halfway house. We freshened up, I gave Axil a feed and we lay down and had a nap. I woke up just in time to get sorted to catch the afternoon train back to Kempsey.

We couldn't make the visit the following weekend because it was Axil's birthday and I had made a booking to have his photo taken. I was sad that Ronny could not be there. He sent us a handmade card with a beautiful bunch of flowers. They were red carnations with baby's breath tied with a pretty red ribbon. I kept those flowers even after they wilted and died, then pressed them into a book.

It turned out that Ronny missed out on most of Axil's birthdays. I'm not sure I would have made it through all the heartache if I didn't have my perfectly beautiful little boy to love and care for. I believe I was a good mum and Axil never went without. He was well taken care of, happy, had all his shots and brought me so much joy – and he still does today.

The months dragged on slowly, but I kept my promises. I visited Ronny on most weekends and sent him fifty dollars every week. I made sure

I didn't leave the house between 11am and 3pm because that was when he could call. We would write each other letters that were so sweet but often demanding. He would write poems and tell me how much he loved me. I was madly, deeply and foolishly in love with him. I could not wait for him to get out and I counted down the days.

When his release date finally arrived, I organised for Angie to watch Axil and I booked a motel room in Grafton along with our return train tickets. I was so excited – my man was getting out! I waited for him outside the jail. He walked out looking so handsome in the new clothes I had bought him. His dark skin glistened in the sun and he grinned at me with his perfect white teeth. I slowly walked towards him. What I really wanted to do was run to him and throw myself in his arms, but somehow I contained myself. He put his arms around me and gave me the biggest kiss. He lifted me into the air and spun me around. I was delirious. The power this man had over me was electric. We went back to the motel where I overdosed again on my drug. I just couldn't get enough of him. He made me feel alive.

We were up early the next day to catch the train back home to Kempsey. I couldn't help but feel lucky – we had been given a second chance.

We settled into home life very quickly. Ronny was the nicest he had ever been to me. He got some work with one of his cousins doing a bit of gardening and lawn mowing. All was good and we were all happy.

Then one day, Ronny asked me if we could try for another baby. I was a bit shocked at the request as Axil wasn't yet two.

"Why?" I asked.

"So our kids can be close together, 'cause we'll be having a tribe," he replied.

I laughed nervously and said, "Okay. I'll give you a month."

I'm not sure what I was thinking. Had I really forgotten I had fallen pregnant with Axil while I was on the pill?

A day or two later, we decided to take a trip down to Sydney to visit Mum and attend the Knockout. It was now late September. Everything was going well for a couple of days, until Mum and I had an argument over Ronny and his pot smoking. I told her to mind her own business and she in turn told me to leave, so I did. I ended up staying with my cousin Macy and her boyfriend Cecil in Eveleigh Street.

Ronny loved the Block at Redfern. He began drinking heavily again, and about two days before the Knockout weekend he went on a drinking bender in a house on Louis Street for two days straight. Meanwhile, I sat on the front fence watching the end of the street, waiting for him to walk out. I suspected that he was cheating on me again and wanted desperately to knock on the door, but I was too scared. I didn't know what he was doing and I never found out.

The day before the Knockout, I went down to the pub to play the pokies. I was thrilled because I won five hundred dollars! Then, around two hours later, Ronny came home asking for money. I didn't have any.

"Yes you do," he said.

"Fuck off back to Louis Street," I replied.

I had planned to go out with the girls later that night, but Ronny wouldn't leave. By 8.30pm the girls were ready to leave and had already jumped into the car, waiting for me.

"You get in that car and watch what happens," Ronny said. I sat back down too afraid to move. I laughed nervously, not sure if he was serious or not. I fiddled with my hair, unsure of my next move.

I then heard him mutter to a girl named Poppy, "I fucking do everything for her and she won't even give me twenty dollars for a stick."

Poppy nodded her head in mock agreement, then she looked at me and mouthed, "Sorry." I smiled at her ever so slightly. Even she was scared. I walked back inside and went to bed.

The Knockout began and we had a great time. Meanwhile, unbeknown to me, Ronny had committed a pub break-in. He jumped the bar, robbed the till and stole smokes and alcohol. By Monday night, after the Knockout was over, the Block was pumping. All the boys involved in the break and enter were at the party, Ronny included. We had a ball.

We decided to head home to Kempsey and I was confused by Ronny's enthusiasm to get back home. He was acting strangely, so I booked our tickets and packed our bags. The ride home was quite enjoyable.

A week or two later, I broke out into hives. The same thing had happened when I fell pregnant with Axil. I thought, *Shit, it's not even been a month yet.* I visited the doctor, and it was confirmed – I was pregnant. Ronny was delirious with joy and I couldn't believe it.

The very next day, Ronny was arrested. He had left his fingerprints all over the pub he had robbed. His parole was revoked, with a few more charges added on, and off he went back to jail. I was left alone again with our son and a new baby on the way.

It wasn't as easy for me to be 'the best jail wife ever' this time because he was moved around from one correctional facility to another. I still gave it my best shot.

Ronny decided to appeal his eighteen-month sentence. His main excuse was our unborn baby. The magistrate asked me when I was due and I told him it was 28 July 1993, so he knocked nine months off Ronny's sentence and set the release date for 25 July, just in time for the birth.

Unfortunately for Ronny, our daughter decided to arrive early, on 18 July at 12.02am. I named my beautiful girl Alyssa Star after my sister and my nan. It was an easy pregnancy and birth. I was only in labour for one hour and seventeen minutes. Ronny rang the very next day. He could not believe she had arrived early. I told him she looked just like him – perfect – and she did. He was due to return home from Parramatta Gaol on 26 July but I didn't see him until three days later. He had decided to stay and party with my Uncle Matt, who had also just been released from jail. When he finally arrived home, I wasn't happy. I questioned him, "What could be more important than coming home to your brand new daughter?"

He had no answer.

My anger subsided as soon as he kissed me. When he picked up Alyssa for the very first time, he cried. He kissed her little face and called her, "Daddy's baby girl." I didn't think I could love him any more in that moment.

Axil was in day care at the Ngaku Multi Purpose Centre, and Ronny asked me when he would get home. Home. Axil attended Ngaku Multi Purpose Centre. The beauty of this centre was the school bus that picked the kids up and dropped them off. I told him Axil would come home soon and as soon as I said it, the school bus beeped its horn. Ronny went outside to collect Axil. When Axil saw his dad he ran straight into his arms. My heart was so full with love and it was one of the happiest memories that I had of us as a so-called family.

We settled into our daily lives. Ronny was like a different man. He was actively involved with the kids. Alyssa would cry for her father. I felt that I was just a titty to feed her. I didn't mind though, as I was blissfully contented.

The happiness didn't last long. The court sent Ronny to compulsory rehab because he had breached his parole by returning dirty urine. As part of his parole conditions, he had to have regular random drug testing. Because his urine came back positive for yarndi (marijuana), his parole was revoked and he was ordered to attend Benelong's Haven, a family rehabilitation centre. He was also scheduled to appear again at Kempsey Court House in six weeks.

Benelong's is an organisation that provides residential services for Indigenous Australians with a dependence on alcohol or other drugs. It provides counselling and courses to assist Indigenous people to address a variety of needs, including physical, emotional, social and spiritual issues that pertain to addictive behaviours. It is also an alternative to jail. Ronny was hoping for this outcome, to stay at Benelong's for six months and not have to return to jail.

During this time, Alyssa became ill with bronchiolitis. She was admitted into hospital where she was also diagnosed with a heart murmur. It was very stressful. Poor Ronny was worried about his daughter, but they wouldn't let him visit. On one occasion, I had to leave Alyssa for about two hours to check on Axil and do the washing. My Aunty Angie was looking after Axil. I'm not sure that I would have coped without her, or Nan and Pop for that matter, during those difficult times.

Ronny apparently rang the hospital during my absence, and when he heard I wasn't there he went ballistic. Later on I tried to explain what had happened, but he was enraged and wouldn't listen to a word I was saying. Thank goodness I wasn't standing in front of him at the time.

Alyssa recovered quickly but would no longer drink my milk. This affected me greatly. I tried to sneak a feed in when she was asleep, but she wouldn't accept my breast, so I started smoking cigarettes again. I told myself, *I have to do something to ease the stress.*

The court day came around, and Ronny wasn't so lucky this time. The judge revoked his parole and sentenced him to twelve months in jail, and I found myself alone with two babies: one two-and-a-half years old and the other five months old. As Ronny kissed me goodbye at the courthouse, he asked me if there was any chance I was pregnant again.

"No," I said. "Why?"

"I don't want to lose you and I don't want you to leave me," he replied. I assured him I wasn't going to leave him – ever. I still carried a lot of guilt. In my mind, I was responsible for putting him in jail in the first place after taking out the AVO.

This time, it was different. I wasn't able to visit him as much as I could during his first jail sentence. Alyssa wasn't a good traveller and she was a sickly baby. I constantly visited the doctor regarding her heart. Finally, we got the all-clear – Alyssa was healthy, and she stayed healthy (thank you God). I decided to lose the weight I had put on with Alyssa as well as attend TAFE at night to study computer bookkeeping and typing. I found so much satisfaction in both activities. I felt it was the first time in a long time that I had a little control over my life.

I still kept up my jail wife duties. I would send Ronny money and visit regularly. It was around this time that I also started looking after Angie's daughter Brittney. Angie had broken up with Brittney's father, Bryce, and had found another boyfriend named Dallas. She was spending more and more time away, so she asked me to take care of her child. Brittney and Axil were very close and attended preschool together, so we arranged that I would care for Brittney. In turn, Angie would come down every second weekend so I could go and visit Ronny at the jail in Grafton. It worked for both of us.

Eight

Second Chances

It was 1994 and I was now a single mother of two taking care of my aunt's daughter and watching over my beloved nan, who was ill. In addition to this, I was attending the local TAFE at night studying for a certificate in bookkeeping and keyboard skills, and still attempting to be the best jail wife that I could. I was not sure how, but I somehow kept it together.

I also found a job as a bookkeeper at Axil and Brittney's preschool. Being so busy helped me to keep my mind from focusing completely on Ronny. I was also able to take Alyssa to work with me, so life was good.

I passed my course and felt a great sense of accomplishment. I had always known that I was fairly smart, but the incident where Miss Jane had called me a cheat for something I didn't do stayed with me all throughout my schooling years. As a result, I never really excelled – I just got by for fear of being called a cheat again.

Obtaining my certificate and graduating from night school fifteen years later was exhilarating for me. I didn't know at the time that education would become an escape – and my saving grace – from the hardships in my life. I felt happy and content. Not only had I graduated from TAFE, I had also lost fifteen kilos, my kids were healthy and happy, I had a job and I knew where Ronny was and what he was doing. Life was good.

Alyssa's first birthday came and went. I suddenly realised that Ronny hadn't made it to the births or the first birthdays of either of his children. It saddened me. His release was quickly approaching. Our love had gone from strength to strength over the twelve months he was in prison so I was looking forward to him coming home.

His release day finally arrived and I had made the necessary arrangements, including booking the train tickets and motel, and organising for Angie to babysit the kids. I was waiting at the gate when he came out of the jail and I ran into his arms. He was so handsome. The love I felt for this man was ridiculous; I couldn't believe how lucky I was. We'd been through so much and survived, and this was our second chance.

We made our way home to our babies. Ronny was unenthusiastic about me working and he'd walk me to work and pick me up at the end of the day. I thought it was sweet until Aunty May, who was the CEO of the day care centre, said to me, "Doesn't he trust you to walk home on your own?"

I'd never thought about him having trust issues with me before, and I smirked as if to say, *Don't be jealous*. Why I would even think that is beyond me now, but at the time that was my mindset. I thought everyone wanted my man because he was so damn hot! Never mind that he was a woman-bashing, drug-addicted criminal.

It soon became evident that Aunty May was right – Ronny did have trust issues. He would glare at anyone who said hello to me, and then give me the third degree. "Who was that? What's his name? How do you know him?" and so on.

Not long after his release Ronny ran into his cousin Bruce, who knew an old footy mate who was looking for players in Newcastle. He asked if Ronny was interested, and he jumped at the chance. Bruce mentioned that the recruiter would provide a house, Ronny would get paid and he could possibly be discovered by one of the major rugby league clubs. Ronny was excited and agreed to go without discussing it with me.

In fact, Ronny was eager for us to move there as soon as possible. I, on the other hand, felt a sense of unease about the situation. He wanted me to uproot our children and leave my job, my family and my nan, who I adored and would never have coped without. I was scared, and every instinct in my body told me, *No, don't go*. But I pushed that thought aside, packed our stuff and asked work if I could take three months leave without pay. This request was denied, so I resigned with a heavy heart.

I made this decision under duress. I really didn't want to go but kept thinking that Ronny had come all the way from Collarenebri to Kempsey to be with me, and that he now wanted to take control of his life in order to look after our little family. I thought he deserved a chance. It didn't take much for me to talk myself into it.

Nan gave me her car – my very first car. It was unregistered, but I didn't care. I was just grateful to Nan. This would make getting around Newcastle so much easier. Ronny packed the car with all our stuff and made the decision to drive to our new house in Newcastle in the unregistered vehicle. I was going to travel down the following week to check it out and then bring the kids down the week after that.

It didn't bother me that Ronny was willing to drive an unregistered car to Newcastle not long after being released from prison. In hindsight, I may have been in the process of becoming immune to his criminal antics. I kissed him goodbye, told him to drive safely and off he went.

After a restless night of worrying about him driving a long distance on his own, he called me the next morning to say he had made it safely. Later that day he called again. He had met with the team manager and settled into our new home. He was excited. He asked me to come down to check out the house and told me his two cousins, Lance and George, would be staying with us.

"Why?" I asked.

He explained that they had been asked to play with the same team.

"Well, why can't they get their own place?" I asked further. "I thought this was supposed to be our house?"

"I've been living with your mob for three fucking years … aren't my family good enough?" he snapped back.

"No, it's nothing like that," I said. "I just thought it would be us. Of course your cousins can stay."

I didn't hear from him again until later the next day, and he sounded strange.

"What's wrong?" I asked.

He explained that one of his cousins had called him and asked if he could pick her up, and that the car had broken down.

"What did you do with the car?" I asked.

"I left it there," he answered.

"Well, go get it. Get a tow truck or something," I demanded.

"I can't. I have no money," he said.

Instead of organising a tow truck, I sent him money. Big mistake! He never got the car. He went and got drunk instead, and I never saw the old blue car again.

I organised for Angie to watch the kids for the weekend and travelled to Newcastle. Ronny came to the train station to meet me. I was wearing dark blue shorts and a fitted cream top. I had made a real effort to look good for him, and by the look on his face when he saw me, it paid off.

"Go on, you looking good," he said.

"For you, baby," I said with a smile, as I gave him a big juicy kiss.

His cousin Bruce was waiting in the car along with his other cousin Lance, who I had met in Collarenebri. Lance was Ronny's first cousin. Their mums were sisters. I liked Lance. He was quiet and polite, and had a real chance of making it before he broke his leg playing for the Parramatta under-21s.

Before seeing the house, we went to Bruce's place. Bruce, his wife and kids were lovely. They had a young son who was sick with cancer. I spent most of the day talking to the little boy and my heart was breaking. We stayed for lunch and then Bruce drove us home.

Our new home was a timber house on a big block of land. We walked up the stairs onto the porch and through the front door. It was very cosy and had three nice-sized bedrooms, a large lounge room and a nice kitchen. The only thing I didn't like was that the toilet was outside near the laundry, so we had to go out through the back door to get to it.

We settled in for the evening when there was a knock on the door. It was Ronny's other cousin, George. It was a little overwhelming being in a house with all these men – not because I felt scared of them, but because by now I knew how Ronny thought. If I looked at one of them for too long, or talked to them too much, I was certain I'd be accused of wanting them.

All three of them smoked yarndi. I'd only tried it twice before – once with my cousin Janelle at the cemetery under the church in Year 9, and the second time just before I met Ronny. On that occasion, I had a smoke of purple heads with my cousin and aunt, and it ripped the guts out of me. It made me feel like I was walking in slow motion and made me so sick that I vomited everywhere. It wasn't watery vomit either – I felt like I was vomiting up Chiko Rolls. That was enough for me. I never touched drugs of any type after that. If yarndi had that effect on me, I couldn't imagine what other drugs would do to me.

I told Ronny this could not happen around our kids, and there would be no smoking cigarettes inside either, so Ronny and his cousins converted a big shed at the back into a 'man cave'. They smoked all weekend in that shed. It was annoying.

Spending the next few days in Newcastle in our new house didn't make me feel like I thought it would. I believed that if I spent the weekend with Ronny, it would ease the apprehension I was experiencing and I would want to move. But it didn't and I didn't.

I moved to Newcastle anyway. I drove away from Nan, my home and my security. I loved Nan so much, and it broke my heart to see her standing there waving goodbye to me and her great grandkids. I couldn't help but think I was making the biggest mistake of my life, but I loved Ronny so much and this was his chance to take care of us, so I left Kempsey once again with a heavy heart.

We settled in quickly. The neighbours had children who were Axil's and Alyssa's ages, which was good. I began playing the 'good little wife' role easily. I was still uneasy about the cousins staying in the same house, but they didn't talk to me much. I soon found myself becoming the handmaiden – cooking, cleaning and washing for Ronny, the kids and his cousins. I didn't mind though, as it kept me busy.

Ronny was going to training daily and playing well. Axil started at preschool for two days a week, which he loved. Alyssa was a happy, healthy little girl who loved nothing more than riding her four-wheeler bike down the steep driveway. All was good.

Aunty Tina was having her twenty-first birthday party in Kempsey and I decided to go. Even though we had only been there for just over a month, I was excited to leave Newcastle. Ronny asked Lance to come as well, so we all travelled together.

It started out as a great night. We were having fun partying, when we decided to go to the top of Middleton Street to another party. Ronny and Lance went to get some yarndi, and Ronny told me to stay at the second party with my cousin Rosie.

He was taking a long time, so I said to Rosie, "I'm going home."

As I was leaving, I got into an argument with a young lad named Rod who was being nasty to his girlfriend Anne, who was also my friend.

"Shut the fuck up," he said.

"Get fucked," I retaliated.

He threatened to hit me, so I said, "I'll get my man to punch the cunt outta you."

Just then Ronny returned and heard me rowing. He walked across to where we were standing and said, "I thought I told you not to move."

Suddenly, he whacked me across my face.

I fell onto the ground and he wrenched me up by the hair and hit me again.

"That'll do Ronny," said Rosie.

He raised his fist to hit me again when Lance grabbed his arm and said, "That'll do, cuz. There's no need for that."

Lance helped me up while Rosie begged me to go with her for my own safety.

Ronny said, "You'd better come home with me now!"

I felt humiliated, sad, angry and confused all at once. My mouth was bleeding and I could feel my face swelling. I was too scared to do anything but follow Ronny home.

As we started walking, Rod ran after Ronny and they started to fight. Rod said, "Come on, big man, your woman reckons you can punch my cunt in."

I secretly wanted Rod to knock Ronny the fuck out, but it didn't happen. A few punches were thrown then it was over as quickly as it had started. Lance and I just stood there and watched.

We continued walking and when we arrived home I went straight into the bathroom to wash my face. I was relieved I wasn't bruised and thought to myself, *My poor face must be used to it.*

As bad a night as it had been for me, it was good for Tina and Lance, who hooked up. Regardless of all I thought Tina had done to me in the past, I loved her as much as I loved my one and only sister. We stayed for another night and then headed back to Newcastle. Tina decided to come back with us. I was relieved to have family and another girl in the house with me.

Our lives seemed to settle for a few months after that. We were all going fine, and Alyssa's second birthday was coming up. My Aunties Mimi and Halle were travelling up from Sydney to help us celebrate. I was excited that Ronny would finally be at one of the kids' birthdays.

The birthday went to plan, and Alyssa had a lovely day. All was going well when something terrible happened. Aunty Halle's daughter Peta, who was two months older than Alyssa, reached up to the bench while her mum was making tea and grabbed a cup. The cup, which was full of boiling black tea, tipped over and scalded her. We all panicked, called the ambulance, and ran into the bathroom to put Peta under the cold water tap. Halle was beside herself. I was not the best person to be around in emergencies, so thank goodness Mimi was there to take control as she always did.

The ambulance arrived and Halle and Peta were taken to the hospital. Peta had third-degree burns to her neck and chest and required skin grafts. It was a very scary time, but she eventually made a full recovery.

Ronny came back from football training wondering where we all were and what the hell had happened. I told him and he responded by saying he felt like a drink.

"Really?" I said. "After what I just told you? And it's your daughter's birthday. Is it really necessary?"

Apparently it was. He, Lance and George went down to the shed and starting drinking. I told them all to sleep there and that they weren't allowed back into the house. I had been brought up around drunks. As kids, we often had to clean up the morning after a big drink-up at Nan and Pop's place, and I knew from experience that children weren't safe in a house of drinkers.

Ronny agreed, and they supposedly stayed out in the shed, or so I thought. In reality, they went out clubbing. Ronny returned home the next afternoon.

"Where the fuck have you been?" I asked as he crawled in the door.

"We just caught up with some footy mates," he said.

I was furious. "You are such an arsehole! You don't give a fuck about anyone but yourself," I said. "You're a father's cunt!"

In response, he grabbed me by my shirt and pushed me up onto the wall, causing Alyssa to start crying.

"That'll do, Ronny," said Mimi, who was watching.

"Fuck you! I'm leaving," I said as I stormed out.

Mimi took the kids outside to play. I started to pack my clothes, when Ronny walked in and closed the door behind him. He looked at me with his steely black eyes and then grabbed me by the throat.

"You want to leave me, do you?" he said. "You want to leave?"

His voice became louder, then he threw me across the room and began pulling all my clothes off the hanging rack, screaming, "Leave then, ya slut, leave!"

I curled myself up into a ball on the floor, too scared to move. He came over to me and pulled me up by my hair. Then he looked me right in the eye and said, "Do you wanna leave me?"

I shook my head with fear and said, "No, no, babe, I don't."

He let my hair go, put his hands through his, and yelled in an angry voice, "See what you made me do? Fuck, Ash, why do you do that?"

I started putting the clothes back on the rack. I could barely get them onto the hangers, my hands were shaking so much. He sat on the end of the bed with his head in his hands. He got up and started to help me tidy up the mess. He touched my hand and I pulled it away. He looked at me puzzled, and said, "Are you right?"

"Yeah I'm fine," I whispered.

He then grabbed me around the waist. I stood straight without responding. He pulled my arms up around his neck. I let them drop. My head was bowed. He grabbed my hands again and ever so gently lifted my face up with his hand. He looked me in the eye and said, "I love you, babe, and nothing or no one's going to come between us."

I looked at him with tears in my eyes. I'm not sure whether they were tears of fear, love or despair, or maybe all three. He lifted my face with his hand again and kissed me softly, and I succumbed to his powers once again, not sure if it was to protect myself or if I was filling myself up with my drug. Either way, I didn't have the power to resist. He took away all my pain in that moment, but only for a moment.

After that, Ronny began to skip his football practice sessions. His manager rang the house constantly. I didn't know where he was going as I thought he was training. One weekend he didn't come home at all.

I was increasingly becoming sick of his selfish behaviour. Ronny had been spending all the money, Lance and Tina were in Kempsey, and

George had gone back home to Walgett. There was barely any food in the house. Fortunately, I had had the privilege of being allowed in the kitchen to watch Nan cook as a kid, and she could make a meal out of nothing. I had learned to do the same. We had a tin of tuna, a few potatoes and some frozen vegetables, so I whipped up some tuna and mixed vegetable patties and the kids gobbled them up.

The next day Aunty Mimi passed through to pick up her son, but ended up spending the week with us. Cayne and Axil were very close. On the day she was ready to leave, I told her I was coming with her. I packed up as many clothes as I could and off we went. I had no idea where Ronny was or what he was doing, and at this point in time I simply didn't care. I was going home to Kempsey to my Nan.

Ronny eventually called me in Kempsey begging me to come back, but I had made my mind up. I didn't like Newcastle and I refused to live there anymore. Ronny's manager and real estate agent kept calling too, to the point where it was becoming annoying. I wondered why they were bothering me, as everything was in Ronny's name. The next time they called, I advised them I had obtained legal advice stating that what they were doing was harassment, and that they needed to speak to their client, Ronny, and not me. My tactic worked – I never heard from them again.

Tina and Lance decided to move to Kempsey too. They drove to Newcastle to get Lance's things, and on their return Tina advised me that Ronny was partying all the time, which didn't surprise me. She also told me he sold one of the paintings that he'd painted in jail so he could go to the Knockout, which was being held in Moree that year. I thought this presented a prime opportunity to remove my stuff from the house in Newcastle.

I returned to Newcastle, packed up the stuff and sent the removalist on his way. I was waiting for Aunty Cynthia to pick me up on her way through when suddenly Ronny walked in the door. My heart skipped a beat.

"What are you doing?" he said suspiciously.

I told him I was going home and was waiting to be picked up. He looked at me blankly and I don't think he believed me. Then something strange happened: Ronny and I had the most honest conversation of our lives. We spoke about how unhappy I was in Newcastle. We agreed that getting Axil to school was far too difficult, and we discussed how Alyssa also needed to be in preschool. Everything was too hard, and – just like that – we agreed that Newcastle wasn't working and we needed a break. He then took me into his arms and made passionate love to me on the lounge room floor.

Cynthia pulled up and I stood up to leave. Ronny grabbed me and held me tight. He kissed me goodbye, and then I walked out. I returned to Kempsey, and Ronny to Moree.

~

I quickly settled back into life in Kempsey and was just beginning to feel happy again when Ronny called from Moree and begged me to join him. I couldn't understand why, until his niece told me he had been with a girl known as Petal. I didn't know who she was or what she looked like, so I started asking anyone and everyone from Moree about her. I soon learned that she was from Moree, had a son and worked at the local employment centre. Ronny had apparently met her at the Knockout and hooked up with her. Not that it matters now, but it did at that time.

I had an overwhelming need to find out everything about her. I had started working at Kempsey Shire Council and decided to track her down. I started calling her daily, asking her all sorts of details about what they did together and how many times they had hooked up. I wasn't doing my job properly because I was too busy obsessing over Petal.

During that particular Knockout long weekend, Ronny committed another break and enter and found himself on the run. He took off to Collarenebri. It wasn't long, however, before he was caught and found himself back in front of the court. Petal went with him. I know this because Ronny's family called to let me know. I didn't do anything and I didn't say anything. I just stayed in Kempsey.

Nine

Drugs, Sex and Violence

Ronny was let out on bail but had to check in to rehab at Benelong's Haven again. His mother rang to let me know he was about to be released again, so what did I do? I stupidly went to pick him up from the train station.

As I approached the station, I saw a tall, dark figure walking towards me. It was Ronny. He had a hoodie pulled over his head. It was dark, but I could recognise his walk anywhere.

He acted like he hadn't seen me, so I pulled up next to him and asked, "Do you want a lift?"

He peered at me from under his hoodie and said, "Sure," then jumped into the passenger side of the car.

As soon as he closed the door, I could smell the scent of cheap perfume. It made me sneeze. I thought, *Arghh that must be Petal's smell.* I didn't say anything, neither did he; we drove home in total silence.

When we pulled up Ronny said he couldn't wait to see the kids. I could feel his excitement. Even though I told him they were both asleep, he walked inside and went straight to them. He lovingly stroked both of their faces and kissed them gently on their foreheads.

"I think we should talk," I said.

He nodded, and we went out to the back veranda.

I asked him what crime he had been charged with and why he got sent to Benelong's. As usual, he denied all responsibility – none of it was his fault. Every time he got into trouble with the police, he insisted that he never did anything wrong; he simply refused to be accountable for his actions or his behaviour, and this time was no different.

Then I brought up what I really wanted to know about – Petal. He pretended that he didn't know what I was talking about.

I looked at him right in the eye and told him, "I spoke to her on the phone and I know everything."

He just brushed it aside, got up and went into our bedroom. I followed him and turned on the light. He took off his jumper and all I could see were love bites on his neck … and he is dark skinned.

My heart hit the ground and I asked, "What the fuck are those things on your neck?"

He immediately bowed his head so I couldn't see his face. I walked over to him and lifted up his head to have a good look but he pushed my arm away. I became angry and started to wrestle with him, and then I became enraged and started punching him. He pinned me to the bed and then practically crushed me with his body weight to restrain me. Then he tried to kiss me.

I pushed and wriggled from underneath him. He was so strong and heavy – I could barely breathe. He then tried to kiss me again, and this time I gave in. My body automatically relaxed; it was like I had been sedated. *Ahhhhhhhhhh … my fix, my drug.* The struggle ended, everything was forgotten and in that instant we were back to where we left off in Newcastle.

The next day, Pop asked me when Ronny was going to rehab, as he was concerned that the family might be charged with harbouring a criminal. On reflection, I think he was sincerely worried for me as he had already made it quite clear that he didn't approve of Ronny. I told him it was fine and that we would not get into trouble. He was not as convinced as I was, and we got into a heated argument. He became very angry and started yelling and smashing plates and cups in the sink and on the floor. I became scared, so I went in the bedroom and told Ronny, "Get the kids. We're going out for a while."

We walked to my friend's place to hang out for the day. We didn't head home until dark. I was hoping everything would have settled down at home by then, and thankfully it had. We all had a grown-up discussion and agreed that Ronny should go to rehab the next day, otherwise he could be found to be in breach of his parole.

The next day, as he prepared to go, he asked me whether I would be willing to move into Benelong's with him. I was shocked by this question and without even thinking I snapped back at him, "No way! I don't have a drug or alcohol problem, so why should I move there?"

Ronny put his head down and mumbled, "I guess."

I almost felt sorry for him. I knew there was no way my kids were ever going to stay in any rehab centre. Ronny settled into Benelong's and I worked my days around him, visiting him three times a week and every second Saturday for Family Day. He did well, and I could see a real change in him.

As the weeks turned into months, I noticed he was becoming restless. We had been talking about moving to Sydney – well, I had been. For the first time since having my children, I really wanted to leave Kempsey. I wanted to do so before our son started kindergarten, and Ronny agreed. Sydney would be a great move for us, or so I thought.

Eventually, rehab became too much for Ronny, so he took off from Benelong's. I had no idea until he showed up at home. He had come to see the kids and me, and advised me he was heading to Sydney. I was shocked and didn't have a say in the matter as he had already made up his mind to go.

Ronny called me as soon as he arrived in Sydney and then began to call me every day for a couple of weeks. Not long afterwards, the calls became less frequent, and I started to worry about him. I began to prepare for the big move to the city. I organised for us to stay with Mum. She was the manager of a hostel, so we had a place to stay. I asked Mum to check out the local schools in the area. As it turned out, there was a day care centre and public school up the road from her place.

This time I was excited to move from Kempsey because I knew it was time for a change. Axil had just started kindergarten at South Kempsey, so if I was ever going to move, it would have to be at this point in time because I didn't want my children moving from school to school as I did. It was my goal to keep them at the one school. Knowing I had a place to live and a chance to spend more time with my mother, I happily packed up all our belongings and off we went. It was early February 1996.

When Mum picked us up at Central Station, she mentioned she had seen Ronny in Redfern looking like nobody owned him, so she had brought him to the hostel, made him have a shower and gave him some clean clothes. I had no idea he was in such a state.

When we arrived at the hostel, Mum told me that Ronny was in the living room. He was asleep on the lounge as I walked in, so I woke him up and told him to come into Mum's quarters.

He quickly jumped up and said, "Gee, it's good to see you."

I looked at him and said, "You too," with a big smile on my face.

He walked into Mum's private quarters and the kids jumped all over him. Even though he spent a lot of time in jail and away from our kids, when he was around them he was always actively involved. He loved his babies and his babies loved him; it filled my heart with hope.

We settled into hostel life and enrolled Axil at Leichhardt Public School, where he would finish his public education. He loved school and made friends easily. Some of those boys are still his friends today. Ronny took him to the South Juniors to sign up to play football with the Redfern All Blacks. We got Alyssa into a day care centre in Redfern for two days a week. Ronny happily took her to school and picked her up. She was only there for two weeks before a spot became available at a preschool just up the road from the hostel. Everything had fallen into place.

I started a job at Mudgin-Gal Aboriginal Corporation, a women's centre run by Aboriginal women, for Aboriginal women. Mudgin-gal means 'women's place'. The core purpose was, and indeed still is, to provide a drop-in service that is safe and culturally appropriate, and to help women with referrals, housing and legal or court support. It also had a laundry and bathroom. I was the part-time bookkeeper for a project that was under the auspices of the centre. It was called Inner West Aged and Community Care, a service being set up in the inner western suburbs of Sydney for Aboriginal Elders. I am proud to say that although the project didn't stay with Mudgin-Gal, a lady named Jeannie Townsend and I worked extremely hard to have this organisation successfully incorporated. Then, due to management difficulties, the project was put on hold. However, Mudgin-Gal asked me to stay on as the bookkeeper and I happily did so. I often say that Mudgin-Gal found me.

It was here that I met a young woman who would soon become my best friend. Her name was Bella, and she lived a similar life to me in regards to being a victim of domestic violence, which at that stage I was still unprepared to acknowledge. Bella had just found the courage to leave her partner. I found strength and understanding in her that I had never seen nor found in anybody else. We instantly became friends, and she opened up a whole new world for me.

Ronny wasn't happy that I was working in Redfern at a women's centre. I didn't understand. He also didn't like Bella or our developing friendship. In early November 1996, Mum, the kids and I visited Aunty Halle for lunch. Halle lived on Vine Street, in the notorious part of the Block that was infamous for drugs and violence.

A local girl, who was a known drug user, was walking down the laneway. As I passed by, she sang out, "Ashlee."

I turned around, puzzled as to why she was calling out to me, and answered, "What?"

"Ashlee, do you know that Ronny's using?" she said.

"Using what?" I asked in my naivety.

"You know using … heroin," she replied.

"Like drug needles?" I asked.

"Yes!" she said.

All of a sudden, I felt dizzy.

My cheeks flushed with heat. I immediately walked up the lane, looking to find and confront Ronny. My heart was pounding out of my chest and my cheeks were burning. I was also hyperventilating and thought I was going to faint. I could smell the filth of urine mixed with smoke in the laneway. There were people scattered and slumped all over the place, shooting up and drinking. Ronny saw me walking up from Vine Street and met me halfway. I looked him in the eye and asked him to show me his arms. My voice quivered as he rolled up his sleeve and held out his arms. There were fresh marks on his arm with little bits of blood.

I felt sick. It was like I was spinning around and around. I said nothing and I turned to walk away. Ronny grabbed my arm and said roughly, "So what, you gonna walk away and just leave me here?"

I shrugged my shoulders and continued walking down that dirty stinking lane. I felt my stomach turn, and the sting of tears in my eyes. I couldn't believe he had stuck a needle into his arm.

I felt a wave of emotion rise within me. As the first tear fell, I suddenly had a memory of my childhood when we were living in Allambie Heights. I had been rummaging through Dani's boyfriend's jacket. He had left it hanging on the doorknob, and I needed to find some money to take to school for lunch. Instead, I found a needle and metal spoon. At the time, I couldn't understand why anyone would have a needle and a spoon in their pocket, but later on I found out what they were used for. I never told a soul for fear that I would get into trouble for looking in other people's belongings. I had the same fear in that very moment. I didn't want to tell anybody.

I headed back to the car where Mum and my children were waiting for me. I tried with all my might to hide my emotions from my babies, but my mum saw straight through me and asked, "What's wrong? Did you see him … is he okay?"

She just kept talking and talking and asking questions until I screamed, "Stop! I don't want to talk about it!"

The car went silent and it stayed that way for the entire journey home. And so my life as the lover of a junkie began.

To say I was confused would be an understatement. I didn't know what to think or feel, I was so messed up. A few days later, Ronny came over to the hostel. He had a shower and went to bed. He slept for nearly fifteen hours; this is known as 'crashing'. When he eventually woke up, I started questioning him. He convinced me he had just tried it – that it was no big deal. I don't know why but I believed him.

Our relationship deteriorated quickly during this time. He was gone more often than not. On several occasions, I walked through the Block and noticed that people were giving me strange looks, or at least I thought they were. I wondered how Ronny could have gotten into drugs. I found out that he had been living it up with a girl named Judy for most of the time he was in Sydney. I was furious, so I went down to the Block and walked up Eveleigh Street to confront her. I offered Judy 'out', meaning that I wanted her to come out and have a physical fight with me on the road. She refused, and Ronny came out instead. He told me to wake up to myself and he walked me to the top of the Block, put me into a taxi and sent me home like I was a little child. I thought it was strange that he was at her house … I was so dopey!

I decided to go out that night to my new friend Rusty's twenty-first birthday party. Most of the hostel folk were there, including a guy called

Jeff, who was very cute. He had light brown skin – a little too fair-skinned for my liking – but he had a really pretty face and a beautiful smile. His hair, which was dark brown and just touching his shoulders, was tied back into a ponytail. He was unshaven and had the prettiest almond-shaped hazel eyes. He was tall, not as tall as Ronny but tall enough, and he had a muscular build. He was pretty for a man. I decided, *If Ronny can do it, so can I.* This was my first attempt at starting something with another man since I had laid eyes on Ronny.

I started to flirt with him in the best way that I could. I wasn't too good at this type of thing, only because I thought that no man would find me attractive. I also only had eyes for Ronny. However, after a few drinks my flirting must have improved because Jeff asked if he could walk me home.

"That's so sweet," I said, and off we went. We barely got halfway through Leichhardt Park when he was all over me. I wasn't sure what I was doing, but I was doing it. All of a sudden we heard voices.

"Shhh, quick, let's go," he said.

He sneaked me into his room upstairs at the hostel, lit a candle and put on some nice music (which must have been his 'getting it on' tape). Things were getting hot and heavy, and then there was this big knock on the door – I almost died. I jumped up and he tentatively opened the door. It was my mother. Someone told her I had left with Jeff, so she came to collect me. Was I embarrassed? Just a touch.

I was petrified that Ronny might find out. I felt so guilty that I went looking for him the following evening. I had decided to have a few drinks with my Aunty Halle at the RSL club. On our way back down to the Block I saw Ronny in the distance. I became fearful, so I ignored him and kept walking. He was good at giving me a quick backhand or grabbing me on the back of my neck, twirling my hair in his hand and forcing me to walk where he wanted to go. He did this more times than I care to remember. I had convinced myself that this behaviour couldn't be regarded as domestic violence. My attitude at the time was, *Oh well, he doesn't bash me like other men bash their women*. I thought I had it good.

I could feel him glaring at me in the dark. I grabbed onto my aunty's arm and we quickly walked back to her place. On my way home, I was waiting for a taxi when Ronny crept up behind me. He had a way of appearing out of nowhere. I would often joke about him materialising out of the shadows and from behind trees, but it wasn't really a joke – he really did.

He asked me what I was doing. I told him I was going home. I began to feel my heart race and I became afraid. I could now sense when he was about to have one of his moments, and this was one of them.

Then something came over me and I said, "Go and hit Judy. She's your woman now. Just leave me the fuck alone."

I started to walk away, when he grabbed me and punched me in my chest.

I lost my breath.

He then started dragging me around by the hair.

Rod, one of Ronny's cousins, ran over and grabbed him and told him to leave me alone. Ronny retaliated with, "You can have the slut!"

From that day onwards, until his sad passing, I had only love and respect for Rod. That night wouldn't be the only time he came to my rescue. I gave him a little smile and ran away to safety.

My obsession, however, didn't waiver, and I couldn't stay away from Ronny. Little did I know that Judy also indulged in drugs. Although I never saw them together with my own eyes, I heard that Judy was pregnant with Ronny's baby. This was heartbreaking for me. I couldn't comprehend it, and I had to go and ask her myself.

I saw her standing at the top of Eveleigh Street lane one day and I just stopped and asked, "Are you pregnant, Judy?"

She replied matter-of-factly, "I was, but I got an abortion." "Why?" The word just flew out of my mouth before I could think.

She replied, "Because Ronny hit me."

"What did Ronny say about this?" I prodded further.

"He just said he would've liked to have known his kid," she said softly and then lowered her head.

The first thought that came to my mind when she told me this was, *He must have really loved her.* It didn't come from the fact that she had had an abortion; it came from the fact he had hit her, just like he had hit me. That thought turned into sadness for her, and then into satisfaction. As distressing as the circumstances for her had been, I walked away content in knowing that she wasn't having Ronny's baby.

A few days later, Axil kept crying to see his dad. Axil was five years old now and had a strong bond with Ronny, so I took him and his sister over to Redfern. With my Aunty Halle we looked everywhere, but couldn't find him all day. Just on dark I said, "Come on son, we have to go."

Axil then asked if we could sleep at Aunty Halle's place that night. I looked at her and she replied, "You sure can," with a smile.

I told Halle that I would go and get something for dinner. Axil insisted on coming with me. Alyssa stayed with Halle to play with Peta, who had healed well from her burns. We got into the car. I strapped Axil into the seat and then we drove along Vine Street onto Eveleigh. As I turned the corner, I saw my friend Nicole. She was holding her new child – her first daughter after giving birth to seven sons. I wound down my window so I could congratulate her and have a look at her beautiful baby. We were chit-chatting for a minute and then Ronny appeared from out of nowhere.

He glared at me. I could see his rage mounting so I whispered, "Go on. Try me. I'll run you over."

Before I knew it, he had pushed Nicole away and grabbed the car door, trying to open it. I screamed and pushed the lock button of the door down with my elbow. I was winding up the window when suddenly he lifted his shirt and pointed to a big shiny butcher's knife protruding from his jeans. My heart skipped a beat, and Axil was scared from hearing me scream. I didn't want him to see the knife, so I forced myself to stay as calm as I could to avoid my son becoming more frightened. I drove off, leaving a trail of exhaust behind. My heart was pounding. I could see the fear in my baby boy's eyes and my heart broke for him. I had never been so scared of Ronny before.

My poor baby boy became increasingly more upset. I believe he could feel my panic and fear. I didn't know where to go, so I drove to Redfern Street to my friend Bonnie, who was at her boyfriend Tom's place. I told them what had happened. They calmed me down and I, in turn, calmed Axil down.

I had to go back to Halle's place to pick up Alyssa. I waited until Axil fell asleep, just in case I ran into Ronny again. At Halle's place I ushered us inside as quickly as possible. I gave Halle a shortened version of what happened; I had become very good at masking the seriousness of Ronny's abuse.

Later that night, I went out onto the balcony upstairs to have a smoke. I just happened to glance down, and there was Ronny staring straight up at me. I panicked and stepped back into the shadows. I couldn't sleep that night out of fear. I was up and down, peering outside. Ronny was there all night, pacing back and forth in front of the house.

The next day, Ronny came into the house looking for Axil. When Axil saw him he was so scared he hid in the corner. The memory of that moment still breaks my heart. I carried an enormous amount of guilt over that incident. I had thought I was a good mother, but every time I recall that memory, I realise that I had failed. As a consequence, I believed that I wasn't a good mother. In fact, I was far from it.

Years later, a counsellor asked me whether there was anything I could have done to change Ronny's behaviour. I thought perhaps I shouldn't have said I would run him over.

"Would that have made the knife disappear?" the counsellor asked.

"No," I answered.

"Then let him own his own behaviour. He did that – not you."

That perspective relieved me of most of the guilt, but not all.

A few nights later, Ronny returned to the hostel. I don't know why I let him back. I didn't even put up a fight, though it wasn't the same. He was coming and going. He'd stay for one or two nights, and then disappear for up to a week. I didn't know what was going on and I was too afraid to ask.

Late one evening on a warm night in February 1997, I heard a knock at my window. It was Ronny. After stumbling through the dark to keep from waking Mum and the children, I opened the door for him. The stink of alcohol and his dirtiness hit me, but I didn't say anything. I knew there was no point. I turned away but then Ronny said, "Babe, wait. Come out here. Somebody wants to see you."

"Who?" I asked, still groggy with sleep.

I turned to follow him down the driveway towards a parked taxi. Its lights were on so I assumed someone wanted to talk to me. I didn't feel scared, nor did I think anything was about to happen. I was dressed in my pyjama shorts and a singlet, and thought for a brief second that perhaps I should go and put on a jumper.

Just then, Ronny turned around and looked me in the face. I thought he was going to put his arm around me or kiss me. I started to giggle, and then I saw his face change right before my eyes; his eyes were cold and dark. My heart began to race as he spat, "What were you doing down the laneway at the Block with another man?"

I looked at him, puzzled, and replied, "What are you talking about?"

"You know what I'm talking about," he mumbled.

Suddenly, he punched me in my face with such force that I fell to the ground.

I felt my top teeth pierce through my bottom lip.

He grabbed me by my hair with both hands, dragging me onto my knees. I put my hands on his, trying to stop him from ripping out my hair.

I was screaming, "No! No! No! I'm sorry, I'm sorry, I'm sorry! Stop! Somebody help me. Mum, Mum, Mum, help me! Anybody help me!"

He then started to hit me in my face. I was screaming, "No! No! No! I'm sorry, I'm sorry, I'm sorry! Stop! Somebody help me. Mum, Mum, Mum, help me! Anybody help me!"

He then continued to hit me in my face.

With every punch he yelled, "You wanna kiss other men."

I was screaming at the top of my lungs, "I'm sorry, I'm sorry! Stop! Stop! I love you. Mum, Mum, anybody, HELP ME!"

I thought somebody would help me. There was a taxi in the driveway with its lights on, so someone must have been in it, and at least twenty-five people were staying in the hostel.

Then I felt an enormous thud on my back – he had started to kick me.

He kicked so hard that his shoe came off. I could feel blood dripping down my face as I was trembling. My voice was hoarse from screaming, and my knees felt like they were on fire. Eventually, he stopped. I tried to stand up, but couldn't.

My next recollection was being pulled onto my knees by my hair and Ronny pointing a butcher's knife in my face. I heard his vicious, slurred and drunken words as he looked me straight in the eyes and said, "I'm gunna gut you like a yellowbelly."

I'm not sure if it was tears, blood or both, but I blinked and with that blink my life flashed before me. All I could think was, *Who's going to look after my babies?*

He let go of my hair and I noticed that he became unbalanced, so I got onto my knees, gathered all my strength, and pushed him over. He stumbled, and I got up and ran for my life, locking the door behind me. Once I was inside, I began to feel weak. I propped myself up on the wall as blood dripped down my body. I made it to the bathroom and turned on the light, singing out to Mum in a panic. She got up and came in to see my face battered and bruised, and blood gushing like a tap from my head. She asked what had happened. I looked at her and said, "Ronny bashed me. I was screaming out to you. Surely to God you heard me?"

"I didn't hear a thing, baby," she said quietly.

I looked at myself in the mirror – I could barely recognise myself. My face was battered and swollen, blood was gushing from my head and mouth, both of my eyes were blackened and my lips looked like balloons.

Mum took control. She grabbed a towel and started cleaning me up. She then rang our friend Rusty and cousin Nick and asked them to come over to take care of the kids while she drove me to hospital.

An hour later, I sat in the emergency department waiting room of Royal Prince Alfred Hospital. I was bloodied and bruised, so the medical team rushed me through and cleaned me up. I had X-rays done and all my vitals were checked. They advised me they would have to shave the front of my hair to stitch up my skull. The doctor said that before they could stitch up my head, he would have to insert his fingers into the wound in my skull to check for glass and gravel. It was the most god-awful sensation I have ever experienced. Thank goodness the wound was clean. I can't recall how my head split open. Ronny may have bashed it onto the brick wall, or maybe it was the result of a kick – I really don't know. They stitched me up and then sent me home.

As I walked into the hostel, all the residents who had been sitting outside as Mum's car pulled up ran back inside. I could hear them talking about me and looking at me through the window as I walked by. I heard them mutter, "Awww … look at her face."

I felt like saying, *Here, have a good look … Why didn't any of you help?* I'm so glad my kids weren't there to see me when I got home.

One of the hostel tenants came to check on me. His name was George. He said, "Ohhh, bub, look at you, I'm so sorry. I heard you screaming."

I looked at him and responded, "Well, if you heard me screaming, why didn't you come out to help?"

He then said I reminded him of his mum when he was a kid, and that all he could do was put his headphones on and cover his head with a pillow. George and I became lifelong friends that day.

I had to make the decision whether or not to press charges. I really didn't want to, but I knew I had to. Mum took me to Leichhardt Police

Station where a very kind and supportive female constable took my statement and photos and assured me that she would accompany me to court if necessary. I went back to the hostel feeling exhausted and in agony; I think I slept for twelve hours straight.

I couldn't stop wondering how Mum hadn't heard me and, worse still, began speculating that she had in fact heard me. She was such a light sleeper that the sound of someone stepping on a leaf would wake her, yet she never heard me scream for her.

This thought was made worse the following night when she woke up at the sound of someone walking up the back stairs. I felt angry.

I said to her, "Oh yeah, you wake up for the hostel guests creeping about, but you couldn't hear me screaming for you," as if it were somehow her fault that Ronny had bashed me.

I dwelled on that for years, wondering whether she was too scared to help, or if she somehow thought I deserved it. I had this belief that Mum liked me being with Ronny because he controlled me – I now know it wasn't her fault.

The police soon picked Ronny up. A girl named Betty, who was a known drug user, came to the hostel to tell me that Ronny was in custody and that he'd asked her to come over to get his keycard. I couldn't understand why he would send her over to get his belongings ... to say I was dopey was an understatement. I lied and told her that I didn't have it. She then asked me how I was feeling. I said I was okay.

"Gee, you made me sorry when he was bashing you," she said.

"What?" I asked.

"Yeah I seen it," she said, "I was in the taxi."

You could have heard a pin drop.

A week later, the police called to tell me that I wasn't required to attend court. Ronny had pleaded guilty to assault occasioning actual bodily harm. The officer advised me that when he was asked if he would care to look at the pictures of me, he declined and stated, "Charge me, I'm guilty."

This somehow made me feel better, because at least he acknowledged what he had done. In my messed-up head, this meant he was sorry. He received a two-year sentence to run concurrently with three other crimes he had committed before the assault.

Ten

Finding the Woman in Me

One would have thought that the last beating would have been enough for me to leave Ronny forever ... sadly, it was not to be the case. He went to jail, the kids and I moved into a flat in Glebe for a month and then into a house in Marrickville where, at the time of writing this book, I still reside. It was during those two years that I became interested in education again. I enrolled at Tranby college to study for a Diploma of Community Development.

Tranby was established in 1958 and is Australia's oldest independent Indigenous education provider. Its mission is to deliver adult vocational education and training accredited courses to Aboriginal and Torres Strait Islander students across Australia.

Those two years were a great time in my life – I was working and studying, my kids were healthy, happy and settled into school and I had wonderful friends. I started going out on a regular basis with Bella and George. We had so much fun together. Needless to say, I was content and free. To celebrate, I decided to get my first tattoo. It was a butterfly, to confirm my newfound freedom.

About ten months later, Ronny's mother, two of his three sisters and his brother travelled to Sydney to visit Ronny. Although he had been writing me letters, I had no contact with him. They pulled at my heartstrings, but I had not responded to them.

Ronny was serving his time at Long Bay Correctional Complex, a maximum and minimum security prison located at Malabar in Sydney. His family didn't know how to get there, so I organised the visit. They asked me to accompany them. I was hesitant, but agreed.

I should have stayed outside, but didn't. We walked in and sat down. The tables were round, so it didn't matter where you sat because you would be positioned directly across from the inmate. I didn't look at him, nor did I speak to him. I could feel his stare though. I was confused. I had the urge to leave, but I didn't.

The visit went by fast. After we stood up to leave and as I walked past him, Ronny grabbed me and gave me the biggest cuddle and whispered in my ear, "I love you."

Without even thinking I responded, "I love you too." He kissed me on the forehead and pulled me close for a cuddle. I nearly cried with emotion, but I somehow contained myself and left.

The next day, Corrective Services called asking permission for my number to be added onto Ronny's phone card, to which I agreed. He called me straight away, and all my good intentions to stay safely away from him crumbled. I wanted to visit him the next day, but he told me I couldn't until the following weekend. I was confused as to why he was blocking me, so I carried out a little investigation. It turned out Ronny was receiving visits from a girl by the name of Yvette. I had no idea who she was, but in my chronic, messed-up state, I considered her to be my competition. I was determined to win Ronny back from her. It wasn't hard – I just made sure that I booked all his visits. Before long, I became his number one girl again.

It was around this time that my sister Lara broke up with her boyfriend Ralph. They had purchased two tickets to travel to America. Their plan was to fly to Los Angeles, then on to San Francisco, pick up a car and drive to the Grand Canyon in Arizona. Due to the break-up, Ralph didn't want to go, and Lara would have lost the money for his ticket so she asked me if I would accompany her. I jumped at the chance. The trip was only for three weeks, so I asked Mum if she would look after the kids. She agreed, and my friend George, who was living with us at the time, was willing to help Mum with the kids. The kids loved George and vice versa. I worried about leaving my babies as I had never left them for more than a weekend. However, I was confident that Mum and George would take good care of them.

Mum was a little concerned about both her daughters travelling alone, so she suggested that my friend Bella come too. Mum was willing to lend the money to Bella to buy the ticket. Bella also jumped at the chance. I was so excited – it was my first overseas trip!

What an adventure it turned out to be. We landed in LA, went outside for a quick look around, then travelled to San Francisco where Lara had arranged for us to stay with our godmother Dana and her husband Will.

Dana and Will were eager to show us around and were wonderful tour guides. We caught a ferry across the harbour to Alcatraz, where we did a tour of the prison. It was so eerie to stand in the cells where the likes of Al Capone ('Scarface') and Robert Stroud ('Birdman') had been inmates. It was amazing. Later on, we drove over the Golden Gate Bridge and had lunch at Fisherman's Wharf, where I tried my first chowder – delicious. We then drove around the hills of San Francisco to Haight-Ashbury, an an old hippy landmark of the sixties and seventies.

In San Francisco I came to the realisation that men found me attractive – African American men in particular. In stating that, I don't want to sound conceited, but the truth was that I never looked at other men and, as a result, I had no idea about the way they looked at me. I was completely oblivious.

On the first night we met some boys, including the first man who helped me to realise I was attractive and sexy. Besides Ronny, he was the only man I had slept with in eight years. I had been intimate with two other men when Ronny and I weren't together, but these short-lived encounters were driven by the need for payback rather than desire.

The first of those two men had been Jeff. The second was somebody I'd sooner like to forget. It happened one night in Sydney when Bella and I went out. We ended up at The Spanish Club on George Street in the city. I was slightly intoxicated and ended up flirting with an African man. We went back to Bella's place, but I couldn't bring myself to do it. I got up and ran home. I had never felt so disgusting in my life, because I couldn't stand the thought of another man touching me other than Ronny. No other man could make me feel like Ronny did; in my mind, we were the perfect fit.

Carl, the American man, was a different matter. He was like candy. He was a tall, strapping young man with broad shoulders, wearing blue jeans and a white t-shirt that caressed every muscle. His smile was dazzling and his skin shiny. I was trying with all of my might not to look at him when he came over and asked me to dance. I nearly choked on my drink and said, "Maybe later."

He kind of tilted his head, smiled and put out his hand for me. Without thinking, I grabbed it. My heart was pounding. I was so nervous. A slow song came on and he put his hand around my waist and pulled me closer. He smelt so good. I melted into his body and could feel every muscle … yes, just quietly, *every* muscle. The song ended and he asked if he could join us.

"Of course," I replied, and we spent the entire night talking and dancing. He was captivating, and I was intrigued.

He offered to drive us home and then asked us to meet up with him the following afternoon, to which we agreed. Lara stayed with Dana, and Bella and I went with Carl. He drove us around and told us about himself and what he did. He looked just as gorgeous in the day as he did at night. I felt giddy with excitement – a feeling I'm not sure I had felt before.

He asked me if I would spend the night with him. How could I refuse?

Finding a place was a little tricky with me staying with the girls and him living at his mother's place. We ended up booking two rooms in a motel – one for Bella and one for us. Bella kicked back and ordered room service and a movie, while Carl showed me how it was really done.

As we entered our room, I could feel my heart pounding and I wondered if he could hear it. The door closed and he turned to look at me. I felt shy and couldn't meet his eyes.

"Are you okay?" he asked.

I replied that I was, and then he pulled me into his arms and kissed me. I was floating. His body was magic. He had me feeling things that I'd never felt before. For such a big man (and I mean big in every sense of the word), he was incredibly soft and gentle. He stroked my body with his fingers, which felt like feathers. It was beautiful to fall asleep in his arms.

I will never forget the way Carl made me feel. He was the first man to really bring the woman out in me and make me feel beautiful. I will forever be grateful to him because he taught me how to tap into my sexual essence – something I didn't even know I had.

We left San Francisco the next day, but not before Bella and I found ourselves in a dither. We had arranged to meet Carl in town for lunch but somehow got lost, which wasn't uncommon for us. We made a wrong turn and ended up in the seedy part of town. A man came walking towards us with something in his hand, which we thought was a gun. We spun around and began walking back to where we had come from, and could hear him picking up his pace. I had never seen Bella move so quickly. I could feel my heart beating faster as I was beginning to panic and break into a sweat, even though it was freezing. After nearly being hit by a tram because we were looking for traffic in the wrong direction, we managed to get safely onto the footpath and hailed a taxi to take us back to Dana's place. I didn't get to meet Carl and was crushed. Although I never saw him again, I'll never forget him. In many ways, he changed my life.

We picked up a Ford Mustang rental car and Lara managed to crash it within the first five minutes of driving. We had to get another car, this time a standard four-door sedan. It wasn't as flash as the Mustang, but a much better choice in my opinion. We travelled south to Santa Barbara and decided to stop in Orange County, where we headed out to explore the nightlife. In our quest to find a 'Black' nightclub, we ran into an African American man who said he knew the best clubs in the area. He said he would take us there if we paid for some petrol, which we did.

The club was a big shed out the back of nowhere with security guards holding sawn-off shotguns. To top that off, the vehicles in the car park were all bouncing and bopping, just like in the rap music videos, and the only other fair-skinned women in the area looked like prostitutes. I have never – and I mean never – been so scared in all my life!

I looked at Bella and said, "If I die tonight, I will haunt you for the rest of your life."

Just then, one of the security guards said, "Goddamn, girl, what you doing around that corner? You're gonna get yourself killed. Get around here."

"Do you have a smoke?" I asked.

"Hold up. I'll get one for you," he said. I was so stressed that I needed one.

The other security guard was screaming out, "Okay, motherfuckers, the party's over!" while pointing his gun everywhere. It was so scary. By the grace of God, a young man came over and started talking to us. He was so nice and offered to take us back into town to our motel.

I asked if he could stop at the petrol station across the street first so I could buy some smokes. Bella and I walked into the store and were looking around when the store quickly began to fill with people from the party – it was a black out! I bet the shopkeeper was scared to death. He was just a skinny little, white dude surrounded by a mass of Black people; it was like being in a movie.

Bella and I hurried back to our new friend Mark's car. What a lovely man he turned out to be. He drove us all the way back into town and dropped us in front of our motel. To this day, I believe someone was watching over us.

We continued our journey. The next stop was the Grand Canyon, and it was there that I saw snow for the first time. About five kilometres away from our destination, we decided to stop to take pictures of ourselves in the snow. There we were, the three of us frolicking in the snow, when a policeman pulled up in his car. We froze. He asked us where we were from and what were we doing, and then promptly told us to 'get the hell back into our car' because a serial killer was on the loose. We never moved so fast in our lives! We jumped back into the car and headed straight to the canyon. We booked into a hotel so we could stay the night and take in the full beauty of this natural wonder the next day.

The Grand Canyon did not disappoint. Its vast beauty was amazing. It had such a spiritual essence that is really hard to describe. The terrain, as well as the shape of the rocks and the valleys that ran through it, were absolutely breathtaking.

That evening, at sunset, we stood outside on a big rock overlooking the canyon. The moon was full; it looked so close I felt I could reach out and touch it. Since that evening, I have never seen a moon as big and as bright as that one.

We continued the next day down Route 66 to Las Vegas. We stopped at the only petrol station on the way to find out it had run out of petrol (or 'gas', as the Americans call it). The man assured us we had enough to get to Vegas and, despite our anxiety at potentially being stuck out in the middle of the desert with a serial killer running amok, he was right.

Driving into Vegas was amazing. One minute, we were surrounded by a desert landscape full of cacti and dust. Then we drove up a hill where we could just make out the neon lights, descended and ascended again, and suddenly it appeared – like the biggest Christmas tree in the world was right in front of us. To me, Las Vegas was as sparkly and as exciting as everyone had ever said it was. We were there for two days and I don't remember much of it. As the saying goes, 'what happens in Vegas stays in Vegas', and that's all I'll say on the matter. What I will always remember, however, is that we had a blast!

After Vegas, we headed off to San Diego, which turned out to be my favourite city of the places that we visited in America. It was there that I tapped into my sexual prowess for the second time. Men stopped me in the street to give me their phone numbers and rolled down their car windows to hand me their business cards. I can't explain it, nor did I understand it. I just smiled, took the cards and kept walking. I felt like a magnet; it was something I had never experienced before and I was not used to this amount of male attention. I was sure it had never happened in Australia – or maybe it had, and I just hadn't noticed. I felt free in San Diego. As Ronny had requested, I sent him a postcard from every city we visited, updating him on our basic activities. I certainly wasn't giving him the heads up on our real adventure.

San Diego was where I met James, who changed the way I thought about myself for the rest of my life. He helped me tap into a power I didn't know I had. He showed me things I never knew existed. I thought Carl was strapping; well, James was even more so. He stood about six foot, two inches with a shaved head, shoulders like a NFL player, and a build that reminded me of a line out of a Salt-N-Pepa song: "A body like Arnold with a Denzel face." Oh yes, he did.

James was a preacher's son, and boy did he have me singing 'Hallelujah'! He wooed me the night I met him, and I stayed with him during the five days we were in San Diego. He sang to me, he gave me his undivided attention and he looked deeply into my eyes with his perfect dark-brown, almond-shaped eyes. He was like sex on legs. He lavished me with full body massages, rubbing me with sandalwood oil. He kissed my feet; in fact, he kissed me from head to toe. Until that day, I had never felt the way James made me feel. I don't know if it was because I had come into my womanhood with a newfound sex appeal, or because I was being adventurous on holiday, but that man made me feel like a woman should feel. He made me feel so good, and all my inhibitions were tossed aside.

I gave myself to this man – completely. Although I didn't love James, he showed me what it was like to be made love to. In a daring moment, I even took a photo of James naked. He was sitting on a stool in all his glistening glory, holding his generously sized penis. I don't want this to sound naughty, decadent or perverted, but it was a beautiful photo of a beautiful man I will never forget.

Many a time when Ronny and I would fight, I would think about James and the photo, which I had burned just before Ronny was released from jail again. I would often lament the loss of that photo. I wish I had kept it so I could have thrown it in Ronny's face when he would start accusing me of sleeping with his mates. In my imaginings, I would have said to him, "I've had bigger and better than you," and actually prove it! Aaaah, James, if only.

With a heavy heart, we left San Diego for LA, where our journey ended.

My sister Lara will never know just how pivotal this experience was in my life. It is because of her gracious generosity that I am the woman I am today. That trip changed me.

We returned to Sydney and I was deliriously happy to see my babies. I had been missing them and they were fretting for me too. We soon settled back into our routine. Not long after, I organised a visit to Long Bay to see Ronny as he was due to be released in early January 2000. It was now August 1999.

The Knockout was coming up in October and I was asked to work in the Mudgin-Gal stall. Ronny was still attempting to control me from prison and he wouldn't have let me go to a Knockout at any other time without him, but I was working and I probably would have gone anyway. My trip away had somehow given me a voice. I was no longer so, 'yes Ronny, no Ronny, three bags full Ronny'.

I went to the Knockout with Bella and our kiddies. That year it was held in Nambucca Heads, so we stayed with my family in Kempsey. The Knockout was great fun, and Saturday was the night to go out. I asked my Aunty Angie if she would mind the kids. She agreed, so Bella, Aunty Halle and her man Claude, Aunty Cynthia, Aunty Mimi and her partner

Frank and I went to the party on the island and heard all the live bands. It was a black out, and it was deadly!

Bella and I went our own way, leaving the couples to do couple things. We had just returned from going to the toilet when we bumped into a local Sydney man named Marley and another lad. Marley was one of Ronny's best mates. He was always kind to me, and when I'd go looking for Ronny he'd always tell me where he was. He would often say, "Don't know why Ronny does what he does when he's got a woman like you." I'd smile and collect Ronny from wherever he was.

This night, I looked at Marley in a different way. He was standing there, tall and golden with his dreadlocks and magical smile. I noticed he had the most beautiful lips I'd ever seen on a man – they were so full and perfect. It took me back to the very first time I laid eyes on him. It was back in 1990 when I had just moved to Sydney, and there was a big day of celebration for Aboriginal and Torres Strait Islander people at La Perouse.

He was wearing blue denim jeans that hung from his hips, a brown, open leather vest that had Aboriginal paintings on it, and cowboy boots and a cowboy hat. He was tall and masculine, with a chiselled jawline and the biggest brown eyes. He almost looked like a Native American – his skin looked like golden honey and he had dreadlocks just touching his shoulders. I stared at him, thinking he was hot and he knew it! He walked past me and smelled good too. He glanced at me, then paraded by as if he didn't notice me admiring him.

It was great to see him. We started talking and flirting. He had such a sexual magnetism about him, and along with my own newfound sex appeal we were like two magnets drawn together.

Marley came home with me that night. We stayed at my Aunty Cynthia's place and spent most of the night talking and laughing. I think we were both mustering up the courage to cheat on Ronny. We then made love, and it was wild and passionate. He was an adventurous lover who liked to please, and he shocked me with his prowess and lack of inhibitions – it was quite the night. The next morning, I woke up with Marley behind me. His arm was tucked tightly around my waist. He kissed the back of my neck and then trailed his kisses down my spine. No one had ever done that to me before and it felt so sensual. He asked me if it was okay if he took a shower. I said sure. I showed him where it was and gave him a towel. Then I started to feel embarrassed and hesitant of what I was doing.

He came out all fresh and we walked out to the front of the house, where he put his arms around me and kissed me passionately. I was shocked. He asked if he could see me later and I mumbled, "Maybe." We said goodbye and I watched him walk – or should I say strut – up Little Rudder Street to hitch a ride. He was one hunk of a man.

Bella and I ended up going back to Nambucca Heads later that day. I was sitting among my friends and family when I felt someone staring at me. It was Marley. I tapped Bella and said, "Look there!" For some reason we both burst out laughing. I looked away, trying to hide myself among my family and play it cool. I didn't want anyone to know what I had done. Ronny would have killed me.

Bella and I decided to go back to Kempsey. We began walking up the hill when a car pulled up beside us and the window came down – it was Marley. He asked what I was doing and I told him I was going home. Then he said something that shocked me. He asked if we could meet up once we returned to Sydney. I looked at him, puzzled, and asked, "Are you sure?"

"Yes I'm positive," he said, and that was how our affair started.

Marley and I carried on our love affair for three months. We would meet whenever we could. I would pick him up or he would rent a hotel room. We would sneak every single opportunity that came our way. We would get it on wherever we could, and I couldn't get enough of that man. I found myself making up excuses to go to Redfern just so I could have him – and he was delicious!

People started to talk, but I denied it. We were extremely careful, or so I thought. I didn't think anyone had seen us being affectionate together in public. We were sneaking around and it was deliriously exciting. Marley was so kind. He would bring little gifts for me, and pick flowers and put them in my hair. He was so smooth to touch. He was a beautiful man, who also happened to be an alcoholic. This didn't bother me because he was so gentle and generous. He was nothing like Ronny.

It all ended on my thirtieth birthday. I had taken a taxi to the Block with my aunties to look for him. Catching a taxi in that area in those days was dangerous. It turned out that Marley wasn't there and had gone out for the night. He had hooked up with an African girl, so that was the end of that. It was magical while it lasted. He did approach me about two days later asking me if there was any chance for us. I looked at him and said, "No, you had your chance, and besides Ronny will be out soon. Let's be friends." He agreed, and we were friends until his passing.

Not long after our affair ended, Marley turned to drugs. I started to think that there was something wrong with me. It seemed every man I touched became a drug addict, as if it were somehow my fault.

Marley passed away in 2013. I was shocked at how hard his passing hit me. I was profoundly saddened by his death. I think it is because he took a little piece of my heart with him when we had our first tryst, and never gave it back.

Eleven

Shame

Ronny was released from Long Bay on 5 January 2000. I wasn't waiting for him to walk out of the prison this time – he was actually waiting for me. He was sitting in the parking lot on a garbage bag full of his belongings. I pulled up and he jumped in. I gave him a lingering kiss, telling him how happy I was to see him, but he didn't seem impressed. I was still in my PJs. He had this fantasy of me running and jumping into his arms, and then us driving to the beach and making love on the car bonnet. That wasn't going to happen.

We drove home not really saying much. It was different somehow, not like before. I knew that he was feeling this too. I couldn't help but remember the adventures I had with other men. I shuddered to think what Ronny would have done had he found out.

We got home and went into my room. Ronny took me into his arms and kissed me so deeply and passionately that I almost lost my breath. He then peeled off my pants and took me. No build-up, no foreplay. It was deep and quick, almost like he was testing me to see if I'd changed my sexual techniques, which might have offered up a clue that I had been with other men. I simply followed his lead for fear of being caught out. Unlike previous times, when we would make love all day and night after he was released from prison, on this occasion it was quickly over. Ronny was excited to see the kids, so he woke them up even though it was only 7am. They were so happy to see him too. After that, life got back to its normal routine. I was working at Marrickville Council in a part-time job, which I didn't really enjoy. In the meantime, Ronny became quiet and brooding, maybe even dark. My mother summed it up well – she said he was like a caged lion in a small area, pacing and moody. I tried my best to do whatever he wanted so as not to rock the boat. I was still petrified that he would kill me, especially if he ever found out about my infidelities. Suffice to say, I wasn't walking on eggshells – I was actually walking on broken glass.

It was around this time that I started gambling. There was a tavern across the road from where I worked that made it easy for me. At the time, I felt gambling was the only private time I had for myself; I didn't have to think about anything, all I had to do was wait for Cleopatra to give me the spins.

One day, I put my entire pay through the machines. I walked out of the tavern in a frenzied state. I started to cry in desperation when I realised what I had just done. My mind began filling with the implications: I hadn't paid the rent, I wasn't sure that I had enough money to feed my kids, and Ronny would be expecting some money. I felt an overwhelming urge to walk out in front of an oncoming bus.

In those moments, I felt as though I had lost my mind and all I could see was darkness. I'm not sure what stopped me because, God only knows, in my mind I had already walked out onto that road. After that day, I stopped gambling on the pokies for many years.

Every day, Ronny would call me at work. He would time how long it took for me to walk home, which was usually twenty minutes. If I took any longer, he would begin to walk in my direction so he could meet me along the way. He was becoming increasingly possessive, wanting to know who I was talking to and what I was doing. Sometimes he would appear out of nowhere when I was in the community for work.

Once, when I was assigned to organise the launch of a project that I had just completed, he came along and drank the wine as if it was water. He even took a few bottles for himself. He became loud and obnoxious, and I was so embarrassed.

As part of my role, I also had to hold meetings at night, which he would insist on attending until one of the councillors complained about him continuously whispering in my ear.

A little bit of relief came when Ronny got himself a job with Leichhardt Council on the rubbish truck. This seemed to lift his spirits. We were both working, and life was improving. Ronny was pleased he was able to contribute towards family life. He was mowing the lawn and fussing about, but I couldn't help thinking that he may have been on drugs again. It was as though he couldn't sit still. His behaviour progressively became erratic, and I could no longer anticipate what to expect from him. It was frightening.

One day, I came home from work to find Ronny hyperactive and sweating profusely.

"Are you okay?" I asked. "Why are you home?"

He started mumbling under his breath, "I wasn't feeling well, so I came home sick." He was washing dishes with sweat dripping, bubbles bubbling and water splashing. Then he roared at me, "You're not worried about me. I'll just keep being your little puppet."

The bubbles from the dishwashing liquid went everywhere as he splashed it about. I froze, not saying a word out of fear that there may have been a knife in the sink. He turned suddenly and started sweeping our already clean floor. I thought, *Shit, he's off his head*. It was like living with Dr Jekyll and Mr Hyde; I never knew who he was or what he was going to do.

Later that day, a strange man came to our house looking for Ronny. I asked Ronny who it was, and he replied that it was a friend from jail. I started to become suspicious of his behaviour and was almost certain that he was using drugs again.

It wasn't long until my suspicions proved valid. Ronny had said he was catching up with one of his mates from work at the local pub and that he wouldn't be long. I called him to see if he was coming home for dinner and he went ballistic on the phone, accusing me of being controlling and jealous. The tone in his voice frightened me so much that I packed the kids up and went to my sister's place, not realising he hadn't taken his key.

Later that evening he started ringing me and leaving threatening messages, and I became scared. It wasn't long before he was standing outside my sister's apartment, demanding that I come down.

My sister's then-husband Bill covered for me, saying I wasn't there.

Then I did the stupidest thing – I walked past the glass doors and Ronny saw me. I saw the look on Bill's face. It was like, *What the fuck! I'm here lying for you and you show yourself. Really?*

I threw the keys down to Ronny. He asked me whether I was coming home. I replied, "No," and stayed overnight with Lara. When I went home the next day, Ronny wasn't there. I tried calling him but he didn't answer, so I locked up the house to try and keep us safe.

A few days later, Ronny pulled up in a car along with my Uncle Matt and they were both clearly off their heads on drugs. Ronny got out of the car and started abusing me. I quickly bolted the doors and windows as he became hysterical. He started smashing pot plants outside, all the while screaming that he was going to kill me. I have no doubt that he would have, had he got a hold of me. He then tried to rip the screen door off its hinges. He was so strong that he actually bent it in half. He began pulling the bars on the windows, trying to rip them off. Then he turned his attention to the windows and smashed the one leading to the lounge room. I was petrified.

Suddenly, everything went quiet.

When I looked out of the window, he was rolling around on the driveway holding his hand, saying, "Quick, ring an ambulance. I'm going to bleed to death." Blood was flowing everywhere. I was terrified, not only for myself but also for my two friends who had taken the kids up the road to buy pizza. If Ronny saw them, I have no doubt he would have tried to hurt them too.

I said, "I'm ringing the police."

Ronny got up leaving a trail of blood, and ran back to the car that was parked on the road with my uncle in it. To this day, I wonder why Uncle Matt didn't attempt to stop him from smashing up the place in his bid to get to me. I lost all respect for him from that moment.

The next five years were the hardest of my life. It was like I was on a nightmarish merry-go-round and couldn't jump off. Each year started off in the same way: we would go out to celebrate my birthday on New Year's Eve. It would always end in the same way too – with Ronny hitting me. Some years were worse than others, but not to the extent of the worst bashing a few years earlier. He continued to physically abuse me, and I continued to stay.

There were also many red flags that foreshadowed what was yet to come. I was caught in a cycle of violence and didn't know how to free myself. I would tell myself, *Well, he doesn't hit me at home, so it's all good.* Furthermore, the kids didn't see it, and he no longer hit my face with his fist, only with open slaps. I figured that this was so I wouldn't show any physical signs of being bashed. On the occasions my face did display evidence of his abuse, I became an expert at camouflaging my bruises with makeup.

During those years, and without my knowledge, Ronny became involved in armed robberies. He came home one night with a bundle of cash, which he said he'd won on the pokies.

"Babe, let's hire a car and go to Collarenebri. Just you, the kids and me," he said, and we did. It was supposed to be for a weekend, but it ended up being for a week.

We hired a white Commodore for the trip. I drove on the freeway and as soon as we hit the country roads, Ronny took over. Even though he didn't have a licence, he was an excellent driver. This trip was the best one of our relationship. On one occasion, I watched Ronny sitting on the banks of the Barwon River in Collarenebri and thought to myself, *This is the happiest I've been for a really long time.* And in that moment, it was.

That night, we decided to go out. I was in such a contented place that I agreed. Ronny, his sister Cindy, his cousin Jack and his girlfriend Molly and I went out together. It was a great night. There was laughter, dancing and singing. The boys even revived their old band, the Redbacks. It was one of the best memories I have of Ronny.

On our way back Ronny and Jack decided to stop at a man's place. The man was called Old Bud, and he hired workers to pick cotton. On the previous night, he had apparently thrown a bottle at Ronny's sister's face, hitting her in the eye. The boys decided that they wanted revenge.

They plotted their attack. Jack was to go and knock on the door to ask about work the following day. Jack followed through, and an elderly lady answered. She told Jack that Old Bud was asleep. Jack just walked into the house, yelling out the man's name. Ronny then ran into the house behind Jack. Together they walked into a bedroom where they found the man lying in bed with his girlfriend.

The rest of us were standing outside the fence, but soon Cindy, Molly and I moved closer to see what was going on. Cindy and I stepped into the house when I saw Jack punching Old Bud. His girlfriend was sitting on the bed, screaming. Another man then opened the door across from the room.

Ronny walked towards him and said, "What the fuck you looking at?" Ronny then hit him and knocked him back into his room, where they started to wrestle.

The second man's girlfriend then jumped off the bed onto Ronny's back, and Ronny yelled out to me, "Babe, get this bitch off me!"

So what did I do? I ran into the house and dragged that poor girl off him by her hair and started punching her. It was brutal.

Cindy spurred me on, "Go on, sister-in-law! Give it to her!"

We started wrestling on the bed, and I became stuck down one side for a few moments. We stopped and looked at each other. I could see the fear in her eyes, the same fear I had in my own. Then Ronny grabbed me off the bed by my hand, and we started to run back to where we were staying.

As disgusting as I feel now about this incident, that night I felt elated, and later on proudly announced to my Aunty Tina that I'd, "just bashed a girl."

Tina looked at me in disgust and said, "She's pregnant you know."

My heart hit the ground. I was sickened to the core of my being. What had I done? What had I become? I was engulfed by a profound sense of shame. In the meantime, the victims had called the police. I started to panic and instantly decided it was time to return to Sydney, so we headed home the following day.

A few days later I had a visit from Newtown police. They asked me to accompany them to the police station. They were going to put me in the holding cell but I asked if I could just sit at the desk because, in my mind, I wasn't a 'real' criminal.

They questioned me and then asked if I would mind being recorded. I did everything they requested. They asked me whether I had anything to do with the assault in Collarenebri and I denied it. I didn't think I had done anything wrong. I was, after all, protecting my man!

Ronny came home later that day and I told him what had happened. All he was worried about was whether I had mentioned his name, which I hadn't because I had told the police I knew nothing about the assault.

A few weeks later, the police caught up with Ronny and he was immediately arrested and put on remand to appear in court. At the same time, I was charged with affray, which is the legal name for disturbance of the peace as a result of street fighting or group fighting in a public place. I was scheduled to appear at the Walgett Court House.

I had to travel by train to Walgett on my own to appear in court. I sat there surrounded by people who were going to court for minor issues that resulted in a criminal record. I was convinced I was going to jail. I was assigned the local solicitor from Walgett Aboriginal Legal Service. He called me into his office and asked me how I was going to plea. I responded, "Not guilty, of course." We then stepped into the courtroom.

The judge asked the solicitor, "How does your client plea to the charge of affray?"

My solicitor replied, "She pleads not guilty, Your Honour."

The case was adjourned to be heard in Sydney.

The police then asked me to be in a line-up. I was in a panic and thought, *A line-up … what the fuck?* I felt like a criminal. I didn't want to do it but my second solicitor, who had taken my case through Redfern Aboriginal Legal Service, told me that it was in my best interest to agree and so I did as she advised.

On the day of the line-up, I made an effort to look good and I dressed as if I was going to work. I was so nervous, I imagined them looking at me through the glass and pointing at me saying, "That's her right there." I was petrified.

At the eleventh hour, my solicitor pulled the plug and there was to be no line-up. She argued that none of the women looked similar to me in any way – some had black hair, some were short, some were super slim, and I was none of these things. She argued these points and said it was a set-up. I was so relieved I nearly fainted.

This infuriated the police officer who had organised the line-up. If it had been the other way around, it would have angered me too; all that work and organising people to go to Sydney for absolutely nothing.

I continued to plead not guilty. In a turn of events, Ronny's sister Cindy gave us all up. She told them I was the main instigator and gave an 'honest' description of what had occurred. I was furious! I felt like dragging her around by the hair. I remember sobbing to Ronny, "Why are they doing this?"

The charges against Molly were dropped, as she had no part in the altercation. Cindy got a bond for affray. I, on the other hand, now faced assault and affray charges. I was assigned a barrister to represent me, who turned out to be great.

In Collarenebri, Jack pleaded guilty and received a two-year suspended sentence. Ronny's and my cases, however, were again transferred to Sydney. I refused to plead guilty. I thought if I did that I would go to jail, and I was concerned about who would look after my kids. I felt like I was fighting for my life. My barrister persisted and advised me to plead guilty, but I continuously refused. I asked him if there was any way I could get out of this. He advised me of something called a 'Section 10'. It is often ordered when the offence is trivial or if it is the person's first offence. Section 10 of the NSW Crimes (Sentencing Procedure) Act 1999 enables a court, on a plea or finding of guilt, to order the dismissal of charges without recording a conviction. If I went for the Section 10, I would have to plead guilty to the lesser charge of affray. My chances of having the charges dropped if I pleaded not guilty would be slim due to Molly, Cindy and Jack being called upon as witnesses for the prosecution. I opted to take a chance on the Section 10 rather than go to trial.

I advised my barrister that I had just enrolled in university to undertake a bachelor's degree in Adult Education and Community Management, and if I had a criminal record I would never be able to teach. The truth was, I had attended an information session where the supervisor and a friend had urged me to sign up but I had not completely made up my mind. After I mentioned this information to my barrister, I saw his attitude change. He advised me to bring my enrolment papers and get as many character references as possible, which I did.

First, I enrolled into the course. Once again, education would be my saviour. It wasn't hard for me to get references because my behaviour during the Collarenebri episode was very much out of character. I'm in no way disputing the fact that what I did was wrong. I got into fights in my time – one being over Ronny and the other over Bella. I was not, by any means a pushover; if someone hit me first then, believe me, I'd hit them back. But for the most part, these physical altercations were few and far between because violence was not a part of my normal behaviour. In this case, I was out of line and it was disgusting. I don't regret much, but

I do regret this incident. In saying that, I would never have learned the lesson I was about to learn had I not done what I did.

~

It was the day of sentencing. Ronny and I had been arguing and I hadn't seen him in a week as we were taking another one of our breaks. We entered the courtroom and his solicitor and my barrister instructed us both to sit in the holding dock. The judge entered and we all stood up. He waved us to take our seats and glared at me through his glasses as he began to read the charges and my character references. After he had finished, he began to speak. He agreed this behaviour was unusual for me and he also believed that I was at minimal risk of reoffending. He then asked me to stand.

I stood up shakily.

He pushed his glasses down his nose, peering at me over the rim of the frames. Then he tilted his head towards Ronny and asked me, "Why are you with this man?"

I stood in silence.

He asked again a little louder, "Miss Donohue, why are you with this man?" He then paused slightly and added, "He's an awful, awful man. Why are you with him?"

I could feel everyone staring at me, even Ronny. I suddenly felt a rush of sympathy for Ronny, who was sitting right beside me.

I looked up. My legs felt like jelly and in a quivering voice. I answered softly, "Because I love him."

The judge shook his head at me, banged his hammer and dismissed my charges with a Section 10. He then called a recess. I slumped back into my seat for a moment, relieved, disgusted, sad and elated. I didn't know what I was feeling. My barrister, however, was ecstatic.

When we left the courtroom, Ronny went ahead of me. We never spoke a word to each other. As I reached the door Ronny held it open for me, however my barrister quickly took a step between us and directed me to walk past Ronny.

As we walked outside, Ronny crossed the road and I could see him doing his little thing with his fingers. It looked like he was counting from one to five, something he would do whenever he was agitated.

My barrister, who was very proud of himself, starting talking to me and warning me not to reoffend. He also spoke to me about a group called Al-Anon; he said I should go as it would be good for me. I thanked him for his help and told him I would look into it, but I never did. What I did do, though, was begin questioning myself about why I was with Ronny. The judge's question kept playing on my mind – nobody had ever asked me that before. In fact, I had never even asked myself. I couldn't answer it because at that point, I didn't even know why. I believe this was my first step towards building up the courage to leave him for good. .

Ronny didn't go back to court. Instead, he began a downwards spiral. It was two weeks before I saw him again. I was starting to worry about him, and I knew I was about to enter into the same pattern as before: we would have had a fight, I would kick him out, then I would start fretting for him. My heart would ache for this man, and then I would search for him or physically place myself where he could see me. It was a toxic and vicious cycle.

This time, Ronny came looking for me to tell me that South Sydney City Council had employed him as a security guard, and he wanted to come back home. He told me his job would be to watch over a new community centre being built on the Block. I was excited for him. He had a new job, and I was accepted into the University of Technology Sydney. Finally, we would be alright – or so I thought.

On the first day of university I was full of happy nerves, not knowing what to expect. Ronny insisted on coming with me so he walked me to the entrance. I was just about to give him a kiss and go inside the lecture theatre when he asked me, "Do you think they would notice if I came in with you?"

I screwed up my face and replied, "I think they might."

I was puzzled by Ronny's request and asked myself the judge's question again: *Why was I with him? Was it really because I loved him? Was it as simple as that?*

Something happened in that moment, and I felt another shift. I think Ronny felt it too. I believe on that particular day, he had a subconscious realisation that he had lost a bit of his grip on me, and I was starting to walk towards my freedom.

Twelve

Round and Around We Go

I started university and a new job within months of each other. I was now employed at Gadigal Information Service as the Community Development Officer. Gadigal is an Aboriginal community radio station that offers a variety of projects. When I first started there were only two full-time workers and five part-time workers. My job was to organise youth workshops called 'Young, Black and Deadly'. These included dance, such as hip-hop and breakdancing, singing, songwriting and theatre. We provided young people with the opportunity to perform in one of Sydney's major theatres – the Enmore Theatre. I loved this project and am still proud to be associated with it as one of its co-creators.

I also took care of Klub Koori, another project that provided Aboriginal and Torres Strait Islander artists with the opportunity to perform at a variety of mainstream venues. It was great fun and I met a lot of amazing people with talent to burn, including Emma Donovan, Christine Anu, Glenn Skuthorpe, Munkimuk, Sharnee Fenwick, Casey Donovan, Coloured Stone, The Last Kinection and Street Warriors, just to name a few.

Gadigal's main focus was the radio station, Koori Radio 93.7FM, which plays only Black music. Specifically, thirty-three per cent is Aboriginal and Torres Strait Islander music, thirty-three per cent is Indigenous music from other countries, thirty-three per cent is African

American music like hip-hop, soul, rhythm and blues, and one per cent is 'white' artists who have collaborated with any of the above.

Gadigal was a fun place to work and employed some remarkable people. My boss, Brad, was one of my biggest supporters, as well as Caroline, who I shared an office with and who taught me all that I know about radio. She was a great listener and heard many of my stories. There was Helen – who I instinctively liked, and was a sister in arms because she had lived a similar experience to me – and Gavin, who provided me with a holistic view on life. There was also Marlene, who shared much of her story with me; Paulette, whose laugh always made me smile; Mark Ross (Munkimuk), who bounced around making up hip-hop raps and was just plain old fun; and Raga – our accountant – whose kindness and 'willingness to help' attitude made the word 'work' seem like a lie.

In the meantime, Ronny was spending more and more time in Redfern, even when he wasn't working as a security guard. There were stories circulating about him robbing banks and post offices again. I didn't know whether it was true or not, but he certainly wasn't giving me any of his money. I was told he had been hitting the drugs hard, too – I was clueless.

A woman named Kara and I were talking one day, as she was going through similar experiences with her man. She advised me that if I wanted to check to see if he had used drugs, I should check the sleeves on his t-shirts, especially the parts that touched the elbow area. If I looked closely, I would see specks of blood. Blow me down Joe, she was absolutely right. I found myself searching through Ronny's pockets and inspecting his shirtsleeves on a daily basis, and I began driving myself crazy.

One day I went to pick up Ronny from work, only to find him hanging out with a woman named Brooke. I asked him who she was, and it turned out that she was married to a Kempsey man and I knew of her eldest son and youngest sister. Stories then started circulating about Ronny and Brooke having an affair. The gossip was that she was using him to sell drugs, and he was using her for drugs. I had no idea, but all I knew was that as much as he was losing his hold over me, I was losing my hold over him.

As I had done so many times in the past, I drove down Eveleigh Street so he could see me. Alternatively, I would walk up to the community centre and make myself visible. Whenever I heard about his dalliances with other women, I never let him get too carried away. This time however, his one or two nights away began turning into weeks and I couldn't cope. I became scared of losing him to these other women. I would feel my body physically yearn for him; I was still addicted, even when I didn't want to be.

One night, I went to the Block after a night out with my friends Bella and Samantha. I was slightly intoxicated and I started a big fight with Ronny. We were arguing over the top of a parked car. He kept chasing me around the car, trying to catch me – we were literally running in circles. My mouth was beyond potty that night as I called him all kinds of names. He had a habit of shaking up a beer bottle or fizzy drink and splashing it all over my face and hair. He did this to mess up my hair and would often do it in front of people. He would often say to me while he was doing it, "I'll make you ugly." He tried it again as he chased me around the car.

I could see Brooke hovering and I turned on her. I told Ronny, "I don't want to fight with you. I want to fight your woman."

"Wake up to yourself," he answered. "You're my woman!"

"No I'm not… that old toothless slut over there is," I screamed, pointing at Brooke.

I heard one of Ronny's friends say to him, "Just hit her."

I turned to the friend and said, "Go fuck yourself."

Ronny said nothing. The next minute Brooke and I started a verbal argument. She was laughing at me, telling me how much Ronny wanted her. I started calling her everything but a woman, and then I offered her out and screamed, "Come on! You and me. One on one, I'll fight you! Come over here you old cunt, so I can jump all over your head." This was how I was talking.

Brooke disappeared for a minute. I think she went to her place to snort some cocaine. I kept swearing at her loudly. Then she was back with renewed energy. She shouted, "Come on then, Ash, I'll fight you."

We started circling each other, both throwing a few punches that missed. A crowd started to form around us. Some people were standing and others sitting on chairs (yes, chairs!) as if we were in a boxing ring. All of a sudden, we were into it. Brooke got hold of my hair and I couldn't get at her. I heard my friend Samantha encouraging me, and then I hit the ground. I heard Samantha exclaim, "Oh no."

Another girl, named Mandy, was then on top of me. There I was, on my back, with two women on top of me – we call this being 'double-banked'. I could hear people shouting, "Give it to her!" or "Get off her!" Each of us had our supporters.

I became infuriated. I kicked my leg up and knocked Mandy off. In the next moment, my niece Liza ran in and pulled Mandy away from me. I seized Brooke by the hair, twisted her around, and started punching her over and over again in her face. I suddenly heard Samantha say, "That's it, Ash," and as fast as the fight had started, it ended.

Brooke freed herself and walked away saying, "That's it. I don't want to fight anymore."

I could see blood dripping from her mouth, and momentarily felt proud that I had made her bleed.

I could hear Brooke's daughter swearing at Ronny, "This is all over you, ya dog. Stay away from my mother!"

I turned around to look for Ronny, but he was nowhere in sight. I glanced over at my friends – they were standing there, shaking their heads. I asked why they never helped me when I was getting double-banked.

"I couldn't," said Samantha. "I got a skirt on."

"You wanted to fight. You needed to learn a lesson," said Bella.

I was angry with them both because I knew that I would never have let anyone double-bank either of them if they ever got into a punch-up.

My phone rang – it was Mum. She said Ronny had caught a taxi to my house to tell her I was at the Block fighting over him. I became enraged, and for the first and last time in my life I drove my car home drunk. To make matters worse, I had Bella in the car with me.

As I was driving down my street, I saw Mum pulling out of the driveway. I followed her and could see Ronny in the front passenger seat. I started flashing my lights for Mum to stop, but she wouldn't. I could see the fear on Bella's face; she must have thought I'd gone crazy. She was probably right.

I began chasing Mum and we ended up back at the Block. Mum let Ronny out of her car and I drove my car straight towards him, over the gutter, trying to run him over. I was furious and got out of the car to chase him down the street. He ran away quickly! I think I scared him, and myself. Poor Bella just sat in the car in shock.

I got back into the car and asked her if she was okay.

"Yes," she mumbled, and we drove straight home.

I didn't grasp the seriousness and implications of my actions until I got home. Mum gave me the third degree about driving under the influence of alcohol and how I could have hurt Ronny really badly or, worst case scenario, killed him. What did I think would happen to me? I didn't argue. She was right. I started to feel sad and sorry for myself, so I took a shower and cried, which is what I do when I'm feeling overwhelmed.

The next day, I packed all of Ronny's clothes and took them over to Brooke's house. I knocked on her door. Brooke opened it only slightly so I could only see half of her. She seemed nervous. I asked her if Ronny was there. She replied, "No, he's not. I don't know where he is."

I heard somebody walk up behind her. I knew it was Ronny.

I tried to look, but she pulled the door tighter so I couldn't see. I didn't have the strength to argue, so I just handed her his bag of stuff and told her to tell him to take my name off any of his legal papers, especially as his 'next of kin'. I'm not sure why I did that, but I did.

I said to her, "He's all yours." Then I flicked my hair and walked away.

This time, I was serious.

Ronny hit the drugs hard and his criminal activities escalated to an all-time high. A short time later, the federal police paid me a visit with a pouch full of photos of men committing armed robberies. I knew not to say anything, even if the pictures were of Ronny. There was no way I was ever going to get up on the stand and identify anybody, least of all Ronny. I could barely bring myself to inform the police he was hitting me, let alone anything else. This wasn't because I loved him; it was a cultural problem that many Aboriginal women faced when living in such relationships. We had such a distrust of the police due to past and present injustices, and fear of repercussion from family, friends and community. More often than not, it was safer to say nothing. I'm in no way condoning this behaviour, but as Aboriginal women putting Aboriginal men in jail, we have to deal with the burden of knowing that they may not get out alive.

Deaths in custody are a reality for any Aboriginal person in jail. Eighteen per cent of men who died in custody between 1980 and 2000 were Aboriginal. The problem has affected society to the degree that in

1992 a National Deaths in Custody program was set up at the Australian Institute of Criminology. Aboriginal deaths in custody have gone up by 150 per cent since Royal Commission into Aboriginal Deaths in Custody findings were handed down in 1991. This is one of the many reasons that many Aboriginal women are reluctant to charge their men – myself included – especially after some of the stories Ronny had told me of his past incarcerations.

Finally, the detectives left. I couldn't wait to let Ronny know about the police investigation. It gave me a legitimate reason to show myself to him.

I hurried over to Redfern to give him the heads up. When I laid eyes on him I nearly died. He was off his face. He was pacing up and down the laneway. One of the boys told me he had been throwing money up into the air. He was nearly unrecognisable, talking to himself as well as ducking and diving as if hiding in the spot he was standing. Everyone could see him. He looked absolutely crazy! The boys said he was suffering from drug psychosis. I tried to approach him and he screamed, "What are you doing here?"

He scared me and I backed away. One of the boys thought it a good idea to give him a shot of heroin to bring him down, as he was off his head on cocaine. I couldn't believe what I was hearing; it was like I was in another world.

I turned around and went to visit Aunty Halle. Not long after, Ronny appeared, still off his head. I went outside to talk to him. He started begging me to let him come home. Every part of my being was screaming, *NOOOOOO!* But I couldn't bring myself to say it so I gave in.

All the way home he kept saying, "Quick, they're coming after me, hurry up," as he dove down into the seat for cover. At one stage, he even wanted me to let him drive, but I wasn't that stupid.

We arrived home, and he began pacing around the backyard. I didn't know what to do, so I just left him alone. He was up for most of the night, striding back and forth and talking to himself. I thought of calling the ambulance, but I didn't know what I would say or if that would trigger a violent outburst.

I didn't sleep much that night. I was up and down keeping my eye on him. Finally, he came inside and went to sleep on the lounge. I woke up the next morning and went into the yard where I found two syringes sticking out of my plants. I didn't say anything because the kids were there, so I hurried them off to school.

On my return, I asked Ronny to come outside. I showed him the needles and told him that if he ever brought any of his drug shit back to my house again, I would call the police on him. He knew I wasn't joking.

I asked him what he was going to do about his drug taking. He said something about 'drying out' and 'going cold turkey'. I didn't believe him. I don't think he believed himself either. Instead, he ended up back at the Block again doing more drugs. I kept going over to get him, and each time I tried to make him stay home or get himself some help, but it was to no avail. He was getting in deeper and deeper.

A short time later, I was in the midst of organising one of the biggest Klub Kooris for Gadigal as part of my Community Development Officer responsibilities. We were showcasing the legendary Aboriginal band Coloured Stone, which originated from Koonibba, South Australia, in 1977. Bunna Lawrie was the band's founder, lead singer and songwriter. Their music blends rock, ska and reggae to produce a unique Aboriginal sound.

This night was a big deal. Everything was going to plan and Ronny was the straightest I had seen him in a long time. The tragedy of the entire situation was that I was working with some of the most prominent Aboriginal music artists in Australia, going to university, taking care of my children and keeping a house all while chasing after my drug, Ronny, who was himself chasing after his drugs of choice – heroine and cocaine. It was a recipe for disaster.

The night was going great. It was a sell-out and there were Blackfullas everywhere. It was my job to take care of the band to make sure that all was well, that they had refreshments, were comfortable and that their requests were met. This wasn't difficult at all because Coloured Stone was one of the nicest bands I have ever had the privilege of working with.

I popped backstage to check on them and Ronny followed me in. He began grabbing the drinks, which were meant for the band. I was horrified.

I told him, "You can't do that."

His reply was, "Well, they just said they don't drink alcohol!"

"That doesn't mean you get to drink their drinks," I said.

He stared at me straight in the face, blatantly picked up two beers, stuffed them down the front of his pants and walked out.

As the night progressed, I was a bundle of nerves. I was trying to do my job, mingle with my friends and also keep Ronny in check.

During the night, Ronny approached me and asked me to dance. The song playing was 'Dancing in the Moonlight', which was one of the band's biggest hits. As we were dancing, Ronny began to act strange. He whispered in my ear, "Why are you dancing like that?"

"Like what?" I said.

"Like that. Do you want everyone to know how you move in bed?"

I looked at him and said, "What?"

Then he swung his hand back, laughed at me and punched me on my vagina.

I walked off the dance floor and carried on as if nothing had happened, hoping nobody had witnessed the incident. I sat down among my friends. Ronny came over and squeezed in beside me when he suddenly began screaming, "What are you doing walking off the dance floor, making a big cunt out of me?" I felt my anger rise and I screamed right into his face, "I HATE YOU, I FUCKING hate your guts!"

Then, out of nowhere – BANG! He punched me straight in my mouth.

My head whipped back and I felt blood pouring from my nose and tasted it in my mouth. My mouth instantly began to swell. I heard the girls gasp. I jumped up, and as I did a bottle came flying past me and hit Ronny's head. I turned to look in the direction it had come from – it was Bella.

Ronny got up and walked out. He strode up to my boss who was sitting with two other performers and screamed, "Youse can have her!"

I felt an overwhelming feeling of shame rise up inside me. I ran to the bathroom, and a few girls followed me and started fussing over me while cleaning me up. I took a moment and then walked back out as if nothing had happened – the show had to go on after all. I walked over to my boss and began to apologise. He assured me that all was fine. I knew him well enough to know he was wondering why I bothered with Ronny. I couldn't answer that myself at the time.

The show finished. I stayed back to make sure everything was okay. I thanked the band and was one of the last to leave.

Everyone was heading to the Block when Bella asked, "Where will we go?"

"Fuck it," I said. "He doesn't own the Block."

By this time, I had decided to get drunk to numb my pain so I could forget what had happened, at least for a little while.

We reached the Block, cruising down Louis Street on foot, giggling and sipping on scotch and Coke when my phone rang.

It was Ronny. He asked, "How fast can two sluts run?"

I answered, "As fast as Forrest Gump."

Bella and I burst out laughing, then we heard a voice behind us yell out, "Well, run Forrest, run."

Bella and I turned around and spotted Ronny standing behind us. We screamed and ran down the street as fast as we could, when suddenly Bella stopped and said, "Why am I running?"

I glanced back and there was Ronny standing at the top of the street and running on the spot. Bella and I looked at each other and burst out laughing even though it wasn't funny. It was simply from the sheer relief that he wasn't trying to kill us. Bella and I took off up Eveleigh Street and ended up having a great night out, swollen, bloodied face and all.

Thirteen

Withdrawals

It wasn't long before Ronny and I were having another one of our breaks. I was sick of him needing to be in Redfern all the time. His behaviour was erratic and becoming ridiculous. I was sending myself crazy watching him and checking his clothes for drug paraphernalia, as well as his shirts for blood marks. I had no idea how bad his drug consumption had become, but I knew that he wasn't straight. His addiction was beyond me now, and I no longer required a reason to kick him out – he would just leave and not come home for days, and then weeks.

About a month after I had last seen him, I returned home from work and spotted Ronny sitting at the table in the backyard. I was startled. I immediately put up my guard and said to him, "You'd better leave before I call the police."

He pleaded with me to listen to him for a minute. He looked terrible. In fact, I had never seen him look so bad. He was once a strapping man, six feet tall and at least 110 kilos. Now his face was gaunt and he looked like he weighed about seventy kilos. He looked like shit, as if he hadn't eaten for a month.

He started begging, "Please, babe, please, I need your help."

I just said, "I don't want to help you."

His eyes were dull and sad. He begged me, "Please, I want to get off the drugs and I need your help. You're the only one who can help me."

I replied, "I don't know what to do. How on earth can I help you to get off drugs?"

He said, "I know how to go cold turkey. I just need you to watch me and help me through it."

I don't know why I agreed and, more to the point, I had no idea what to expect or what was in store for me. I asked him when the last time was that he used drugs and he said that morning. I asked him whether he had any drugs on him and he said no. I then let him come into the house and told him to take a shower. I got some of Axil's clothes for him. Axil was now twelve years old and as big as his father. I also made Ronny something to eat. He seemed okay at first. There were no obvious symptoms of withdrawal. Later that afternoon, he started to sniffle a bit and then began sweating, and I thought, *Oh, this isn't too bad.*

I made dinner, fed the kids and prepared their things for school the next day. The kids were asleep, so I showered and got ready for bed. Ronny seemed fine. I had set up the lounge room for him. He asked whether he could sleep in my room so I could watch over him, and I thought to myself, *Oh yeah, I see what you're doing.* As it turned out, even if I had wanted to get intimate, he was in no condition to perform whatsoever!

At about 1am, it began. He started kicking his leg out twitching and wriggling with pain. I didn't know what to do. His nose was running profusely, and then he started crying and projectile vomiting. It wouldn't stop. He then said that he needed to go to the toilet and all three excretions happened at once – it was like attending an exorcism. I was so scared.

His bodily twitching escalated and something oozed out of every orifice. His leg kept kicking out. It was the most horrific thing I have ever seen in my life. Then it subsided for a short time, as if we were in the eye of a tornado and we went back into the bedroom.

A short time later it started again, but this time he was too weak to walk so I carried him into the bathroom, put him on the toilet and ran a bath. I took his clothes off him, helped him into the bathtub and proceeded to gently wipe him down with a washcloth. He had big tears streaming down his face. For the first time, I saw such hurt and pain in his eyes. I wondered to myself what had happened to this man to make him so self-destructive. More importantly, I had a quiet realisation that there would be no need for me to ever seek revenge on him, because no matter what I could potentially do to him, I would never be able to hurt him as much as he had already hurt himself. He was dancing with his own demons and I wasn't even on the dance floor.

Out of sheer necessity, we spent most of the night in the bathroom. The next morning, he was able to hold down a cup of tea. My mother joined forces with me and pumped him full of vitamins. I suggested we go to the beach. I thought the ocean had the power to fix everything, and he agreed. He was still slightly twitchy and he would sigh all the time. His nose was also still running and he looked so sad. We had a quick swim at Maroubra Beach then drove to La Perouse for some fish and chips before going home.

Ronny laid on the lounge and I placed a bucket next to him as he was still in a bad way. I asked him for Brooke's number so I could call her, as I thought she might have a Valium or something to help him settle down. He was reluctant to give me her number, but I needed help as I didn't know what to do and I knew that she would. I called Brooke and gave her an update on Ronny. She was shocked and told me she would be over soon.

While I waited for her to arrive, I quickly tidied up. I'm still not sure why. She eventually knocked on the door and I let her in.

She took one look at Ronny and said, "Look at you ... you look like death warmed up," then handed me some tablets. She advised me to give him two every four hours. I didn't know what they were. I was too scared to leave the room in case she gave him some other drugs, so I just wandered to the kitchen to give them a little privacy, but I could still keep my eye on them.

When I talked about this incident several years later, many people were shocked that I had asked Brooke for help and had let her into my house. The truth was, Brooke was the only person who kept Ronny alive when he was lost in his drug habit. It was Brooke who made sure he had a feed and a shower and watched over him. Once I got over my jealousy, I felt a sense of gratitude towards her for keeping him alive

It took a week before Ronny recovered as much as he could. He started eating again and began getting some colour back into his face. He began to look better than he had in years. I spoke to him about the idea of going home to Collarenebri for a while.

He said no, because he wanted to be with the kids and me, and so the cycle continued.

After that, Ronny barely left the house. I started wondering why he wouldn't venture out. I asked him and he just said that he didn't want to go anywhere. I thought it was strange, so I started asking around. It turned out the police were still looking for him regarding some armed robberies, and there was a first instance warrant out for his arrest, which meant he could be arrested at any time. It suddenly struck me that for the first time in our relationship, and after everything we had been through, I felt like he was using me.

Life became increasingly unbearable. He didn't want to go anywhere and he also expected us to stay at home. The kids and I were climbing the walls. He would watch my every move and call me constantly. I began to feel like a prisoner in my own home. I started to feel resentment towards him. He was putting our lives in danger in order to keep himself safe, so I had to do something.

My mother was living with us at the time and worked for Corrective Services. I tried to talk to her about the situation, but she refused to get involved and no one could blame her. I felt trapped and claustrophobic, as we couldn't go out or do anything.

One night, we were all sitting on the lounge watching television when we heard a big knock on the door. I opened the door and came face to face with the police – our house was surrounded. In the interim, Ronny had run down the hallway to hide and my mother stayed in her room.

The police asked whether they could come inside and take a look. I knew my rights and answered, "Do you have a warrant?"

They replied, "No." I told them to come back when they had one, so they left.

Later that night, Ronny sneaked off to his cousin's place.

The police returned the next day with a warrant and promptly ransacked my home. I have never felt so violated in my life.

A week passed, and Ronny thought it was all clear so returned home. I had enjoyed the glimpse of freedom and felt resentment upon his return. Life went back to normal – dropping the kids at school, going to work, picking up the kids from school and going home and staying there. I was becoming annoyed and depressed. I could see the effect that this was having on my children. To this day, I'm constantly surprised that my kids turned out as well as they did, as my choices were quite questionable. I tried to talk to Mum about how I could get Ronny out of the house, but she wasn't much help. Then I thought to myself, *I'll ring the police*. And that's just what I did.

On Monday 4 August 2003 after dropping the kids off at school, I stopped at a payphone on Livingstone Road and rang Crime Stoppers. I told them I would like to report a criminal who was wanted by the police. I gave them his full name and told them he was hiding in Marrickville at a particular address. I also asked if the police could please arrange to get there between 9.30am and 3pm. I didn't leave my name – I just hung up.

My heart was beating so fast that I thought I was about to have a heart attack. I quickly jumped back into the car, got myself together and went home as if nothing had happened. I continuously checked the doors and listened for any little sound.

No one came. I thought, *Fuck, what now?*

That evening, I had to drop my friend Melanie's son home from Little Athletics. I called into home first to grab something and out of the blue, Ronny decided to come for a ride. We headed towards Crystal Street in Leichhardt. At the crossroad of Canterbury Road the lights turned red. I looked to my left and there was a big black car full of police officers in SWAT gear. Ronny saw them too, and then glanced at me and mumbled, "Get fucked."

I said, "What?"

He told me it was the police's 'special response' team in the black van. I became scared and nervous.

Ronny then told me, "Calm the fuck down and act normal." The lights turned green. The black van followed us as we drove. My heart was beating rapidly as we turned into Melanie's driveway. Before I knew it, the police jumped out, guns and all. They wrenched open the passenger door, pointed their guns at Ronny and asked, "What's your name?"

He replied, "What's your fucking name?" Then he added, "You already know who I am."

I jumped out trembling and got the boys out of the car. Melanie ran out and took them inside and I rang my mother, screaming.

The police asked me for my name, what my relationship to Ronny was, and so on. Then they handcuffed him. He asked if he could say goodbye to me, so they let him. I put my arms around him and sobbed onto his chest. He kissed me gently and said, "I love you, babe," and off he went.

I went inside, thanked Melanie and told her how sorry I was that this had happened at her place. She assured me that everything was okay. I thought, *How dare I put that onto another person and her child?* My selfishness during that time never ceases to amaze me.

The following day, five police officers came by. I was petrified that I would be charged with harbouring a criminal. They questioned Mum at length too, and I was scared that she might get into trouble given where she worked.

The commanding officer asked her why she didn't feel the need to do anything about the situation at hand or why she didn't call the police. He was upset by her behaviour and advised her that a report would be sent to her boss about her lack of action. I felt a sharp twinge in my stomach and wished I hadn't called the police. The commanding officer placed me under pressure with question after question. Unlike my mother, I became a blubbering fool. He soon picked up that I was the person who had called the police. He asked me whether I had called Crime Stoppers. I burst out crying and said yes, and fell sobbing onto his chest. I told him I was scared and wanted Ronny out of my house, but hadn't known what to do so I had called Crime Stoppers. The commanding officer gave me a little hug, assured me I had done the right thing and left.

We all went back inside. My mother angrily asked why I hadn't told her that I had called the 'fucking police'. I replied, "Because it was anonymous."

She was furious, screaming about how it could jeopardise her job and wondered what on earth I had been thinking.

I looked at her and said, "I was thinking about our safety and my sanity, that's what I was thinking."

We didn't talk for a few days. The commanding officer followed through with his threat and notified Mum's boss. It was all sorted out, thank goodness, and there were no repercussions. Ronny had no idea I had called the police, and I never told a soul. Only Mum knew, so we just picked up from where we had left off. I was so relieved, and I felt free.

Remarkably, when Ronny appeared in court a week later, he got bail. I swear that man had more lives than a cat! When the judge said he was free to go, I thought, *Oh fuck. What now?*

Ronny was so happy. I pretended to be.

We went to pick up the kids, who were at the park with Melanie and her kids. When Axil, now thirteen, saw his father, he ran into his arms. Alyssa, who was eleven, followed. Melanie shook her head and said, "Gee, you're lucky, mate."

Ronny stayed off the drugs to the best of my knowledge. We were getting on well, so decided to go to Collarenebri for Christmas, and it was actually one of the best Christmases and New Years' we ever had.

Our happy little bubble was about to pop again, however. One morning at Collarenebri, I was hanging out clothes on the washing line, when Ronny came up to me and said, "What are you doing?"

I answered, "What do you think? Hanging out clothes."

He then said, "Yeah, sure you are. I know you're posing around for David."

I was confused and said, "What?"

David was Ronny's cousin who lived three paddocks away. I just shook my head and started walking towards the house when all hell broke loose!

He grabbed me by my hair and started dragging me around. I put my hands over his hand to stop him pulling. His little eighteen-year-old cousin Mandy came running to my rescue, screaming, "Stop, cuz, stop!"

Just then, his mother and sisters came walking up the driveway. I rushed towards the front door. He chased after me and put his fist up to hit me. His mother screamed at him, "Leave that girl alone, you big bully!"

I got inside safely and was surrounded by my Aunty Tina and her partner Lance.

The next few days were tense and he would constantly watch me. Tina asked me to do her hair and I agreed. Ronny got angry because he wanted me to lie down on the couch and watch a movie with him. I said I would do so after I finished Tina's hair. He then started carrying on like an idiot. He fell to his knees, exclaiming to Tina how much he loved me but I didn't love him back. It looked and sounded as if he was having a mental and emotional breakdown – it was scary.

That night, he had another episode and smashed the front window of my car. I thought, *Shit, he's going to smash my car up. How will we get home?* I started to plot my escape. I sent Axil up to Tweed Heads with Ronny's cousin Beryl, so that just left Alyssa and me. I packed my bags but made it look like I was sticking around. I put only twenty dollars worth of petrol in the car as I was too scared to fill it up in case he figured out what I was up to. Finally, my opportunity arrived. He told me he was going to have a shower. I put out some fresh clothes for him. As soon as I heard the shower running, I grabbed my packed bag and my handbag, ran out, threw it all into my car and drove to where Alyssa was jumping on the trampoline. I screamed at her to hurry up and get into the car, but she didn't want to get off. I thought, *Oh fuck*. I screamed out to her again, "Hurry!"

She must have heard something in my voice because she then jumped straight off and into the car. I drove the back way, as Lance and Aunty Nola had drawn me a map of how to get out of there on the back roads. I thought that if I went the back way then nobody would see me. My heart was pounding. Once I was on the road, I was too scared to look back.

We finally got to our first stop at Gulargambone. Tina called me to tell me one of Ronny's cousins had just driven into town, and was surprised to see Ronny at his mother's place because he had just seen my car go out of town. Tina said Ronny became furious and started abusing her, Lance and Aunty Nola. He had then stomped down to his mate's place and tried to drive off in his car, but it hadn't started.

Alyssa and I made it safely back to Sydney. I arranged for Axil to fly down two days later and, finally, we were all home and safe.

Our life got back to what we knew as normal. I was no longer walking around on eggshells, having to watch what I said or defend myself for briefly looking at anyone. I used to joke to my friends, "Gosh, he goes on as if every man wanted me."

We may have laughed, but it was not a joke as his jealous outbursts were terrifying. There were so many times when I thought he would hurt me like he did that time at the hostel. I was still haunted by that night. It stayed with me throughout our entire relationship. Even though the extent of his violence never again reached that level, I felt trapped in the fear of it happening again.

About two weeks after my escape from Collarenebri, Bella called me. She said, "Guess what?"

I said, "What?"

She said she had just walked into the pub up the road from home, and saw Ronny sitting there playing the pokies with Brooke. My heart dropped and an uneasy feeling came over me. *Fuck! I thought he'd stay in Collarenebri.*

It turned out that Ronny asked Brooke to drive out and pick him up. He gave her a sob story that I had taken off and deserted him without warning, and he didn't know why. God only knows what else he said. Brooke, however, cared enough for him to go and 'save' him.

I began thinking that everything we had gone through in recent months was proving to be pointless. I had helped him to fix himself up, and now she was going to help him mess himself up again with the drugs. In the end, helping him to withdraw had been for nothing, and I came to the realisation that I couldn't compete with drugs.

Fourteen

The Other Woman

I stewed about Ronny being with Brooke and began getting progressively angrier. I thought, *You're not going to get him that easily*. My default game of 'you're not woman enough to take my man' began yet again. I placed myself in locations where he would see me. Lord knows what I was thinking, because I didn't – I just jumped back onto that merry-go-round.

Ronny returned home again. Everything was going well until 26 January 2005, which was Australia Day for most Australians but Survival Day or Invasion Day for Aboriginal and Torres Strait Islander peoples. We call it that because it's the anniversary of the arrival of the British.

The Yabun Festival was held annually on this date. Yabun, meaning 'song with a beat', is an event hosted by Gadigal Information Service – Koori Radio 93.7FM. It's a festival highlighting Aboriginal and Torres Strait Islander performers. There is a variety of food, dancing and singing, children's activities and stalls for merchandise as well as information from government and community organisations. It's a wonderful event that showcases just how deadly Aboriginal and Torres Strait Islander people are and how far we've come … we have survived!

I had been working all day and Ronny was hovering, watching my every move. It was hot, and I was hot and bothered. The line-up that year was amazing. I didn't really want to go to the afterparty as I could tell what mood Ronny was in. However, he insisted we go and I agreed simply to avoid arguing. I chose not to drink as I simply wasn't in the mood. He, on the other hand, was drinking everything in sight. I noticed that one of his friends gave him something that looked like a pill. I asked him what it was. He merely replied, "What was what?" I said, "That pill your mate just gave you!"

He acted dumb and made it appear as if I were seeing things.

A musician, who quite fancied me at the time, was performing. Somehow, Ronny found this out and kept walking back and forth past him at the after party. I thought, *Fuck! I had better get out of here.* I told Ronny that I wasn't feeling well and wanted to go home, but that he could stay if he wanted to.

He stared silently and lethally at me. My heart began to race. He then said, "Why? So you can meet up with one of your fucks?"

I told him to wake up to himself. To dissipate the tension, I placed all my focus back on to him and ended up staying. About fifteen minutes later, as we walked through the crowd onto the dance floor, we spotted Ronny's cousin Maryanne's boyfriend pushing her around.

I said, "Do something, Ronny."

Ronny walked up to the bloke and said, "You better watch yourself, mate," and then, without warning, king hit him in the mouth. The man stumbled backwards.

I screamed, "What the fuck are you doing, Ronny?"

He replied, "You told me to do something, didn't you?"

I thought, *Fuck this! I'm off.*

I couldn't explain why I was willing to help another woman in the same situation, but not myself. More to the point, I couldn't explain why I would ask Ronny to do something about another man's violence when he himself was violent.

As I learned later, this scenario isn't uncommon. Over the years, I witnessed many violent men hit other men for bashing their sisters, aunties or even mothers.

I added sarcastically, "I'm going home. You can come home too if you want, but you look like you're having so much fun!"

He snarled at me and said, "Let's go then."

We walked outside and Ronny suggested we take a short cut through the Central Station Devonshire Street pedestrian tunnel, which is an underground walkway that links Elizabeth and Chalmers Street to Railway Square and George Street. It's about 300 metres long.

He was quiet, but I could see him flicking his fingers as if counting from one to five over and over as he walked, which I always took as a warning signal of his rising fury. I started feeling nervous and slowed down so I was walking about three steps behind him. As soon as we entered the tunnel, he started abusing me and calling me 'slut guts', which were his favourite words for me, accusing me of being with various men. He didn't stop berating me. I peered ahead to see if anyone was further up in the tunnel, but there wasn't a soul in sight. At any other time of the day or night, that walkway would have been filled with buskers and people walking in both directions, but not that night.

I began to panic. I thought, *Fuck! If he gets into me here, nobody will hear me, nobody will be able to help me. Fuck ... he could kill me and no one would know.*

I started talking calmly to him, agreeing with most of what he was saying, trying to talk him down. It took all my inner strength to stop myself from crying as I was so scared, and what generally takes ten minutes to walk seemed to take hours.

We finally made it to the end and walked up the steps. I sighed deeply with relief. Ronny asked a man who was standing on the street for a smoke, but the man refused as he only had one cigarette. Ronny asked for a draw of the smoke and the man refused again. Then – slam! Ronny punched him straight in the face and the man fell to the ground. I panicked and ran across the road.

I could see Ronny looking for me so I tried to hide but it was too late. He saw me and I saw him smirk. I thought, *Fuck, what am I going to do?* I saw a 7-Eleven and ran inside. I pulled out my keycard and quickly bought him a packet of smokes. As I turned around to leave there he was standing right behind me. I was shaking with terror. I passed him the cigarettes and said, "Here, babe, I bought you your own smokes." He seemed to relax after that.

I hailed a taxi. Ronny stood in the shadows so he wouldn't spook the driver. Many taxi drivers didn't pick up Aboriginal people so we often had to improvise in this way. On that particular night, I wouldn't have picked Ronny up either – he had anger written all over his face.

We jumped into the taxi and Ronny started snickering under his breath. He then grabbed me by the back of my neck and twirled my hair in his hand – this was his favourite move. He started shaking my head, telling me that I made him sick and he was sick of the way I treated him.

He asked me whether I wanted my head smashed through the window. I thought, *I hate you, you dickhead!* I must have pulled a face or something because he banged my head against the window. He grabbed the side of my waist, pinching my skin and demanded, "Look at me!"

I looked at him, really looked at him, and there was not a tear in my eye – only resentment. He then said, "Do you love me?" As he asked this, he put his hand around the back of my neck, drawing my face closer to his.

He asked me the same question again. I looked him straight in the eyes and said, "No! I hate your fucking guts!"

He grabbed me by the front of my throat and banged the back of my head against the window. I wondered what the driver thought and why he didn't stop to kick us out or why he didn't say something. Clearly, Ronny wasn't about to accept my answer. He sat back in his seat and sulked all the way home. I just sat quietly and still before stepping out of the taxi. I couldn't wait to get inside my home.

Once we were indoors he started yelling at me. I walked down the hall and felt a thump on the back of my right ankle; he had thrown one of his size eleven shoes at me. This action triggered something in me. As a child, my mother would throw her shoe at me when I was being naughty or cheeky, and then tell me to bring it back to her. I felt something inside me snap, but kept walking to my mother's room for safety. I woke her up and asked to use her phone. She handed it over and I called the police.

I walked back out and told Ronny, "You'd better leave. I've just called the police on you."

He said, "What for? I've done nothing. There're no marks on you," and he laughed.

He then stood up as Axil came out of his bedroom. Axil was now nearly fourteen. He took over the situation and told his father to shut up and go to bed. Ronny tried to push past Axil, but Axil shoved him up against the wall. I suddenly had a realisation: *What was I doing? I was supposed to be protecting my son, not the other way around!*

The police turned up and I let them in. They looked at Axil who was opening the fridge in the kitchen, but I said, "No, no. That's my son. Ronny's the one on the lounge."

Ronny was pretending to be asleep. He slowly stood up and they escorted him away. He was still laughing, saying, "I'll see you in the morning, babe ..."

I thought, *No you won't, 'babe'.*

I did see him in the morning though. I had packed his bag with everything he owned. It was waiting for him on the back step upon his return. He knocked on the door. I answered and all he said was, "Are you going to send me back to this life?"

I looked at him and said, "You've been living it all along," and I closed the door.

My phone soon began ringing off the hook. It was Ronny leaving messages.

One was, "I love you."

Another one was, "I'm sorry."

The next one was, "You wait, ya slut," and so on.

Later that day, the sergeant from Marrickville Police Station stopped by. I told him about the phone calls and he advised me to take out an AVO, so I did. The police issued an interim AVO.

I attended Newtown Court House a few days later to formally apply for the AVO. I was sitting in the waiting room when I saw Ronny striding up the steps. Fear swept over me and I froze for a second. Then a woman who knew both Ronny and me said, "Quick, Ashlee, go in the safe room."

I ran to the door and knocked on it quite hard. I heard Ronny scream, "You think that door will stop me? I'll kick that cunt down!"

I ran inside, slammed the door behind me and huddled into the corner, shaking uncontrollably. *He must have come to contest the AVO*, I thought. I was petrified when my name was eventually called. The security guard escorted me into the court, and Ronny wasn't there.

The judge promptly issued me with a five-year AVO.

Fifteen
Secrets

I barely saw Ronny during the year. However, I would hear stories about him. He was now apparently sharing himself with not only Brooke, but also a white girl named Ann. I tried not to let the stories bother me but in all honesty, sometimes they did. I even once turned on Ann, chasing her with a stick up the laneway. I had enough sense to not let Ronny back home, but I made sure all his other women knew that if I wanted him, I would have him.

Having said that, I did make some progress. I stopped looking for him and checking up on him; it was like I'd thrown in the towel.

The year went by quickly, and before long it was 26 January 2007. I was still working at Gadigal and it was time again for the Yabun Festival. I went down the Block to park my car at my aunty's house. I saw Ronny out of the corner of my eye in a laneway and something just came over me. I was suddenly filled with rage and hate. He looked dirty and skinny like a full-fledged junkie. I walked up to him and started to abuse him, shouting at him to get himself some help, if not for himself then for his kids. I called him selfish and self-centred and hurled the following question at him, "Do you want your kids to bury you before your time? Do you?" He just ignored me and ran away.

Later that afternoon, my Aunty Halle rang to tell me that Ronny had overdosed on the Block. He had died for a few minutes. The ambulance had to give him a shot of adrenaline in the heart to bring him back to life.

One of my greatest fears was that he would die doing drugs and I would have to tell my babies; it nearly manifested that day.

I drove straight over to the Block to search for him. I walked down the laneway, asking everyone who came my way whether they had seen him. I knocked on the door of his cousin, where he generally stayed. A girl answered the door and I asked her if she knew where Ronny was and whether she knew anything about him overdosing. She said yes and mentioned that it had been scary because he turned purple. I then asked her what addicts generally did after overdosing. She looked at me with shame and replied, "Go and have another shot!"

I couldn't believe what she had just said. I thanked her for her honesty and walked away in a daze. As I retreated, she sang out, "Go and try Brooke's."

As I approached Brooke's place, I saw Ronny peering at me from behind a curtain. He quickly stepped away. I knocked on the door. Brooke answered. I asked her to let Ronny know I was looking for him. She told me he was not there. I told her I just spotted him at the window. She denied that it was Ronny. I began pleading with her and telling her he had nearly died, and I just wanted to make sure he was okay. She just looked away. In that instant, I put my hands up and said, "Fuck it! I give up. If he wants to be a junkie and kill himself then so be it," and just walked away.

I spent the rest of that long day working at Yabun and had tickets to the afterparty that night – I needed a drink after all that chaos. I asked Aunty Tina and her partner Lance if they wanted to go with Bella and me, and they agreed.

As we neared the venue at The Gaelic Club in the city, Bella said, "Careful, Ash, there's Ronny."

I pretended not to see him and continued on. Lance stopped to talk to Ronny while Bella and I went into the Gaelic Club to get our party on. Lance came in and asked if I had a spare ticket for Ronny. I told him I didn't.

As the night progressed we caught up with my friend Melanie. Upstairs was hectic so the five of us sat on a table downstairs where it was quieter. We were rowdy, the music was pumping and Blackfullas were everywhere. We were drinking and laughing and having fun, when I felt someone staring at me. I turned towards where I felt the gaze was coming from. It was Ronny. He was sitting on a stool at the end of the stairway that led to the disco area.

With my alcohol-induced confidence, I decided to go and see what he was doing. My friends tried to convince me not to worry about him or talk to him, but I didn't listen.

I went over and said, "Hey."

He replied, "Get away from me."

"What do you mean?" I asked.

"Go over there to all your friends," he said.

"But I want to talk to you," I answered. "I was so worried about you today."

Although he was filthy dirty and off his face on some kind of drug, I still saw remnants of the man I had fallen in love with all those years ago.

Annoyed at his attitude I said, "Oh well, if you don't want me, I'll just go find a man who does."

He looked at me and asked, "Why would you want me, Ash? Look at me."

Even he was confused as to why I would still desire him. I looked at him, puzzled. He saw this and realised he still had me.

Then, in a booming voice, he said, "Just try and go with another man in front of me and see what'll happen."

In all the madness stood two addicts: one severely addicted to alcohol and drugs, and the other just as addicted to the addict. My heart ached so much that it hurt. I was damaging my children, my family, my friends and myself – over and over. I had hurt my heart, mind and body for this man's love. I had endured the beatings as well as the verbal and mental abuse. My addiction had been just as harmful on my own soul as his had been to him.

I knew this now; I knew he was no good for me. We were no good for each other. I didn't want him back, yet something inside me was resisting and overriding my newfound awareness. I was fighting a constant battle on the inside and was too afraid to throw in the towel completely.

In my sickness – the sickness of this toxic love addiction – his threats were the only words I wanted and needed to hear. In my world, Ronny's words meant that he still loved me.

Ronny and I rejoined my friends. As we sat down, I saw the look on the girls' faces, but again chose to ignore their concerns. The alcohol continued flowing, the conversations were getting louder, and we were having fun. By then, I had lost all my self-respect. I could tell by the look in my friends' and Aunties' eyes that I was losing theirs, too, but I couldn't stop. I was hungry for him and had an overwhelming need to have him, which was all I could see. I drank more than I usually did that night to keep myself from seeing what was really in front of me – a broken-down junkie. I was never a good drinker, but I needed to feel good about myself and so I drank and drank and drank some more.

It came to closing time and we all decided to kick on. We started walking through Belmore Park towards the Block to attend the 'after' afterparty. All was going well until I decided to ask Ronny some questions that needed answering. I began to rant in my drunken state and verbally abuse and accuse him of all sorts of things. Then I suddenly blurted out, "Oh well, you're probably only hanging around for Tina!"

Then all hell broke loose. I hadn't spoken about this in years, yet here I was, opening old wounds. All the resentment and unfinished business I had bottled up inside me from years ago came gushing to the surface.

"What?" Lance asked, and turned to Tina.

"Yeah, Lance, don't you know Ronny and Tina had a thing?" I said.

Suddenly, Ronny headbutted me and my head flew backwards. I looked him straight on and said, "You make me sick, you piece of shit!" and slapped his face as hard as I could.

"Fuck this! I'm going," said Melanie storming off.

Bella came to my rescue, as she had done so many times before. Then somehow, in all the confusion and accusations, Tina wanted to fight Bella.

"Go away," said Bella, and she walked away.

Tina and I started arguing and swearing at each other while simultaneously stating our love for each other through our tears. Lance and Ronny stayed at a safe distance, not wanting to hear or know what was going on, but watching transfixed nonetheless.

Tina and I plonked ourselves down on a park bench out of sheer exhaustion. Out of nowhere, in that moment of silence – and for reasons that I still don't understand – through my sobs and tears I blurted out to Tina, "I was molested by Pop."

"What?" she exclaimed in shock. "Don't lie."

"I'm not," I said quietly.

"You lying cunt, I'm not sitting here, listening to this shit!" she spat out, and I heard her singing out to Bella saying she was going to bash her as she took off.

I was stunned. I didn't know what type of reaction I was hoping for, simply because I had no idea that I was going to tell her what I did. All I knew was that this wasn't it.

Lance and Ronny followed Tina, and I was left alone on the park bench feeling betrayed, abandoned and unheard—just like the first time I had told someone what had happened.

~

My mind drifted back to Pop. He was the only father figure I had ever known. The first time he molested me I was nine years old. We were coming back from a weekend at Stuarts Point and all the kids were in the back tray of a ute with Pop, ten in all. Nan was driving and Mum was in the front seat.

Uncle Floyd was sitting near Pop and they were leaning their backs onto the cabin. We were all covered with blankets as it was just on dark and getting cold.

"Anyone want to swap places?" Uncle Floyd asked."Yeah I will," I said.

I swapped places and sat next to Pop, and Uncle Floyd moved to the back of the ute.

At this time I had no fear of my pop. He was kind and loving and sometimes growled at us, but hey … he was Pop. All of us were crammed in, but it kept us warm. We continued driving along the highway, and some kids dozed off while others were wide awake. Occasionally, the wind would blow the blankets up so we had to hold them tight.

A few moments passed Pop said to me, "Give me a little feel."

I looked at him in confusion. He said it again, "Let me have a little feel," as he slid his hand down the front of my pants. I only had on a pair of shorts and a t-shirt, and I felt his large, rough fingers as they touched the bare skin below my belly. My stomach flipped with nervousness. I froze with fear for a moment and then screamed at the top of my lungs.

"No!" I protested and started banging on the glass trying to attract Mum or Nan's attention. I looked for help from the others in the ute. One of the others saw what was going on and the look on her face saddened.

We made eye contact only for a second before she huddled back down under the blanket.

I looked back at Pop and said, "I'm telling on you."

"No one will believe you," he said confidently, and it turned out he was right.

I moved away from him. Pop was groping around under the blanket, feeling our legs. He grabbed my leg and asked, "Whose leg is this?" When I replied it was mine, he let out an evil snicker. I curled up next to whoever was near me and forced myself to go to sleep. From that moment on, sleep became my coping mechanism.

After that day, I did everything possible to stay out of Pop's way. Some days were harder than others. He would often sit on a chair near the front door and wait for the girls to walk by. Then he would pretend to slap them on the bum or grab at them. One day he grabbed at one of my female relatives as she walked past him. I saw him reach for her private parts, but she kept running. I was about eleven at this time.

I said in disgust, "I'm not walking past you," and ran down the hall and the back stairs to get out of the house.

We never spoke about his behaviour – we pretended it wasn't happening.

I finally spoke up in the summer of 1980, when I was twelve years old.

Pop sneaked into the bedroom I shared with my Aunty Cynthia. I was fast asleep, and I woke up to find his hand down in my bloomers. I was shocked and terrified, with my eyes blurry from my sleepy state, and I jumped up in the dark and screamed, "No, stop! Stop! Who's that?"

I realised it was my pop. "I'm going to tell on you!" I shouted.

He laughed and stumbled out of the room. I'm not sure if he was drunk or pretending to be. I'm also not sure if my Aunty saw or heard what had happened.

Nan heard and sang out in a concerned voice, "What's wrong?" I walked into the hallway. By then, my great-nan, Nan and Mum were huddled together outside my room. They had woken up from the sound of my scream and had come to see if I was okay. Four generations of Donohue women stood there, looking at each other, searching for clues about what had just happened. The mood was heavy and the hallway was dark, except for the light that streamed in from the bathroom. We all stood in a circle. They glared at me and I suddenly felt scared, sad and vulnerable, and then began to cry.

"What happened?" asked Mum.

I told her that Pop had put his hand down in my bloomers.

She asked if it was the first time. I lied and said that it was.

Nan was furious and said to Mum, "Put the police on the old cunt."

My great-nan dropped her head and shook it in shame. She sighed deeply then started tut-tutting. I was told to return to bed and lock the door by putting a knife in it. That tactic wouldn't resolve the situation as he would simply corner me elsewhere. He only tried to touch me a few more times after I told them. I think the only reason he stopped was because I got my period. Nothing was done, nor was it ever spoken about again until 26 January 2007, on that bench with Tina.

After that, Tina made it her business to tell everyone about my confession. The family travelled to my other aunty's place in Newcastle to discuss it. Out of my seven aunties, it is my belief that only a few didn't believe me – namely, the two I was closest to.

When they all came to visit me to discuss 'the situation', none of them ventured inside my house. When I walked outside to greet them I felt like that twelve-year-old girl in the hallway again – stiff with fear of my truth.

Aunty Mimi was the only one who spoke with me about it.

She was the one who was the most sceptical.

"We know this stuff happened in our family, but not by our dad," she said.

She glanced at her sisters, sitting around the table and I didn't respond. The tension was so thick that I could barely breathe. It felt like I was on trial. The aunties who didn't believe me were bursting out and condemning me, while the others stayed silent, not really saying anything or making eye contact. They just sat there.

In my heart of hearts, I knew that they knew I was telling the truth, but no one had the courage to stand up and take my side. I had once felt I belonged in my family, but after that incident I never truly felt part of it again.

Pop and I, however, worked our way through it. This was sparked by Pop's stint in jail for domestic violence. He was sixty-four years old at the time, and I decided to write him a letter in the hope that somehow I could free myself from this burden and he would finally understand the impact of his behaviour.

Dear Pop,
I'm writing you this letter while you're in jail because I know you are sober and have a clear mind.

I need you to know what you did to me as a young girl has affected me greatly and was wrong, and how much your actions hurt me and damaged my life.

I know that you probably won't ever admit to what you did to me, but that doesn't make it right or my fault. It's wrong, very wrong. And I also know it wasn't just me, I saw you touch other girls and they more than likely saw you touch me too.

You made me think it was my fault. Well, it wasn't, it was yours. You are nothing but a dirty old man that touches little girls. Do you know what they do to people like you in jail?

Firstly, let's get something clear. If anyone in our family asks you about what you did to me, from now on you better tell the truth, because I'm telling you that if you don't, I will charge you and I will subpoena every girl that I know for a fact you touched to testify against you. This is no joke. I carried this around for years thinking somehow I deserved it and I somehow did something to make you do it to me, like it was my fault ... it was NEVER my fault, it was always and will always be YOURS, so I'm done with the shame and I'm giving this back to you. I don't own this GUILT, YOU DO!!! I did nothing wrong, YOU did.

You made me feel unsafe in my own home. I hated locking my door, but when you would visit I would put my daughter in with me and lock my door. That's the effect you had on me. Do you have any idea how you made me feel the very first time you touched me? I was a little girl who loved and respected you! You turned that love into fear, shame and betrayal.

How do you think a little girl would feel when her grandfather tried to touch her private parts? Did you somehow think that was okay?

I am so sad by all of this. You have been the only father figure I have ever known. You must know what you did was wrong.

Your actions make me feel like I no longer belong in this family since I spoke out about it. All because you couldn't keep your hands to yourself.

I hope someone finds out about you in there and you get what's coming to you.

Ashlee

I didn't see Pop or any of my family again until later that year at my Aunty Claudia's wedding; I was actually surprised by the invite. It was a beautiful ceremony and a wonderful reception. I was supposed to go back with my sister Lara and her husband Bill, but decided to stay, and I'm glad I did.

Pop was at the wedding. He didn't leave my side that night. I said, "It's okay, Pop."

He sat near me, looking sad. He looked at me and said, "I'm sorry for what I did. I love you like you're one of my daughters. I'm so sorry."

I again said, "It's okay, Pop, it's okay."

He admitted that what he did was wrong and apologised. That was all I needed to hear, and in that moment I found forgiveness.

He passed away in 2011.

Sixteen

For Old Times' Sake

It took me a while to get over the initial shock of my confession as well as the subsequent feeling of being rejected by my family. It really shook me up.

I decided to get some help – real help. I began to attend counselling sessions that focused on dealing with the aftermath of being sexually abused. I also started tiptoeing around the periphery of my relationship with Ronny. After working with my therapist I began feeling a slow internal shift, like I was no longer scared to say how I felt or what I thought. I had found my voice, and I was ready to speak out and stand up for myself.

I think Ronny intuitively realised that I was done with him because he no longer had the same power over me. I was healing, while he was diving deep into despair; we were no longer walking on the same path of addiction.

Then, one evening after attending a boxing class at the Elouera Tony Mundine Gym, I walked out to find a tray of sandwiches and cut-up fruit in the boot of my car.

I looked at Bella and asked, "What's all this?"

She told me Ronny had brought them for me.

I said, "What the fuck?" and took all the food out of my boot.

She said he was wondering whether I would let him come home. He had also joked that I must have been watching *The Biggest Loser* because I was going to the gym. I laughed because I thought it was funny, and then it struck me, *Why had Bella talked to him?* And I asked her the question.

She replied, "He looked like he needed someone to talk to."

I screwed up my face and said, "Let's go!"

As we headed back to Marrickville from Redfern, we stopped at a set of traffic lights. I looked ahead and saw Ronny in a phone box. My stomach felt as fluttery as a butterfly. I thought to myself, *I bet he's ringing Alyssa*.

Sure enough, when I returned home Alyssa said, "Mum, Dad just called. He asked me to ask you if he could stay here for a few nights. He wants to sort himself out and then go home to Collarenebri."

I looked at my beautiful, innocent daughter and said, "Alyssa, I really don't want your dad here anymore."

She began pleading with me, "Please, Mum, what if something happens to him and we do nothing? I won't be able to live with myself." My heart ached for my baby.

I was fuming, thinking, *You lowdown dirty dog, manipulating my daughter for your own needs*. He knew his emotional blackmail no longer worked on me as I was no longer scared of him. Instead, he used the same tactics he had used on me in the past on his own teenage daughter.

I looked at her and said, "Okay, Alyssa, but if he comes here you have to be prepared to have your stuff stolen and your heart broken if he doesn't follow through with his promise to you."

She nodded and said, "I know and I'm willing to deal with it. I love Dad. I just don't want anything bad to happen to him."

Ronny called back and Alyssa told him it was okay to stay. He was knocking on our door within ten minutes, which made me think he was so sure of the results of his manipulation that he had already made his way to Marrickville. Alyssa made a bed for him in the lounge. Funnily enough, I slept soundly that night.

The next day, I got the kids ready for school. Ronny was sitting outside having a coffee and a smoke when he asked if I would take him to a particular place where he could get onto the Brup program. I had no idea what he was talking about. He said it was a medication that would help him to get off heroin, without withdrawing. The medication was called Buprenorphine. It is integrated into a program that helps heroin addicts to wean off the drug without the horrendous withdrawals. It relieves drug cravings without producing the 'high' or dangerous side effects of other opioid programs. I agreed.

For the first time in my life, I felt extremely embarrassed to be seen with Ronny. I felt like everyone was saying, *God, is she back with him again?* I lost the magic filter that had somehow made me oblivious to all the stares and gossip around me where he was concerned. It was like I could hear and feel everyone's judgment – even my own. Ronny, however, seemed pleased with himself. He fulfilled his promise to his daughter, so I was relieved.

The night before he left, he tentatively came into my room. He sat on my bed and thanked me for helping him. He told me how much he loved me, and that he was sorry for everything he had done. I don't know why, but I fell for it, one last time. I resisted slightly at first, and then allowed him to take me into his arms. I knew in my mind that I shouldn't, but my body wouldn't listen. I won't say we made love, but we did have sex. It didn't matter what state that man was in, it was like he knew exactly where and how to touch me. He had the ability to bring my body to life, even when his was only half living. He slept with me that night, and it would be the last time we ever shared a bed.

I woke up early the next morning to get him to the station. We were up before the kids, because I didn't want them to think we were getting back together. Ronny and I drove to Central Station and walked hand in hand to the train. As he jumped on I stood back nervously, wished him a safe trip and asked him to take care of himself. He looked at me and said, "Come here."

I moved in closer and he grabbed my face in his hands and gently kissed me. His kiss became increasingly more passionate, but I felt a shadow of sadness pass over me. I knew it would be our last kiss, and it was.

I felt a sense of relief as I left the train station. As I drove off, the song 'Kiss and Say Goodbye' by The Manhattans came on the radio, and I burst out crying. I knew it was the end, I wanted it to be the end, but I had loved him for half of my life. Every other time we ended our relationship or had one of our breaks, I always knew deep down that it wasn't over, but this time I knew that it finally was.

About six weeks went by and I was studying hard, finishing my degree while my workplace was moving offices to Redfern. Life was busy, and busy was good.

One morning, I woke up feeling terrible. I felt nauseous and my stomach was churning. I went to the bathroom and nothing came out, my heart stopped. *Fuck! When was my last period?* I rushed out to the calendar I kept on the dining room wall only to realise that I was two weeks overdue! My head started spinning. *Shit! No, no, no*, I kept thinking. I dashed to the chemist and bought a pregnancy kit. Back at home, I quickly took the test, and the results were positive. I became numb and thought, *What am I going to do? I was finally free ... Shit! Shit! Shit!*

I decided to visit the doctor to make sure it was absolutely positive that I was having a baby. I had the required blood tests and a few days later I went back for the results. It was confirmed – I was pregnant.

I walked away from the doctor's room in a daze. I just couldn't believe it. I looked up to the sky and asked God, "Why did you give me this baby?" I was almost pleading, "Why didn't you give it to somebody who wants it?" I began to cry.

By this time, Ronny had returned to Sydney with his cousin Jack. I think he had to appear in court. I was trying to stay out of his world, so I didn't know this for a fact. However, I still called him and told him I was pregnant and having an ultrasound that day. I then asked him if he wanted to come. He was ecstatic and thought it was the best news he had ever heard. He told me he would be over in twenty minutes, and he was true to his word.

Ronny walked in through the back door. I stood near the dining table and he took me in his arms and gave me the biggest cuddle. He then dropped to his knees, put his hand around my hips and kissed my stomach. I stood frozen to the spot, my head spinning. *I can't do this again*, I thought to myself and began to cry. Ronny jumped up. I think he thought I was crying with happiness as he then began to cry, too. I buried my face in my hands and leaned into his chest.

We went for the ultrasound. This was the first time Ronny had ever accompanied me or taken an interest in the medical exams, and the first time he had heard the heartbeat of one of his babies in the womb. It was an emotional moment.

We drove home, not saying much. I think Ronny was overwhelmed with what he had just experienced. We went inside and he didn't stay long, which was fine with me. He told me he and his cousin were heading back to Collarenebri the next day, but he would stay if I wanted him to.

I told him to go back and reassured him that I would be okay. We would figure out what to do after I passed the twelve-week stage. I also asked him not to tell anybody. That night I cried myself to sleep.

The next day came, and my mum and her best friend dropped by. We sat at the table and I just blurted it out: "Mum, I'm so sorry, but I'm pregnant." I'm not sure why I apologised. My mother was over the moon. She had always wanted more grandchildren. I started crying again, and she suggested we go shopping. We drove to the Bonds factory in Stanmore and headed straight to the baby section. It was all too much for me and I simply wasn't coping.

A few weeks went by and morning sickness set in, which was difficult as I had never experienced it with my other pregnancies. I was still trying to come to terms with having another baby at the age of thirty-six and thought, *Okay, I can do this*.

Soon afterwards, I travelled to Gosford with my boss Brad to organise a 'Young, Black and Deadly' workshop. It was good to get away to clear my mind. During the trip I noticed some dark spotting, which looked like old blood. I started feeling scared and realised I could lose the baby.

I prayed to God again, "Dear God. I'm sorry about what I said before. I do want this baby. Please don't take it from me."

The next day I went straight to the doctor. I had a blood test and then the doctor ordered an ultrasound. My HCG hormone levels had dropped drastically, and the ultrasound showed an empty womb. I was in the process of miscarrying at eight weeks. I was devastated and in shock.

It took several days for my little baby to pass completely out of my body. I cried the entire time. It was extremely painful and emotionally devastating. Many of my female friends and family members had told me that when they miscarried, they didn't feel anything and it was like a normal period, just heavier. Mine wasn't like that. The pain was excruciating and felt like I was going into labour. I lay in the shower all night until the hot water ran out.

I was distraught and cried for days. I rang Ronny and told him. He said he thought something was wrong because I wasn't answering his calls. The truth was I didn't want to hear his voice. I started to blame him, telling him it was all because of his drug taking and every other thing he ever did wrong. He just listened and told me he was sorry as I sobbed my eyes out.

Later on I apologised to him, and told him what my mum had previously said to me, "Baby, it's nobody's fault. Its little spirit just wasn't strong enough."

I still didn't feel better, as I blamed myself for saying that first prayer. I learned a very valuable lesson out of this experience. I thought, *Be careful what you pray or wish for, 'cause it just might come true.*

I wasn't sure where I was going or what I was doing. I was quite messed up. I kept in contact with Ronny, but the phone calls decreased from daily to weekly. I then learned he had a new girlfriend, whose name was Louise. She was only seventeen years old – the same age as our son. I called him names and was disgusted and I let him know as much. Once again I felt him slipping away and I started asking myself, *Do I have it in me to fight for him again? Do I really want to? What was I fighting for?* I think it was just the emotions of losing the baby. I felt that I somehow owed him something because I had lost his child.

In the past, whenever we had argued I would say to him, "Tell me you don't love me and I'll walk away for good." He never would. Instead he would always say, "I'll always love you, Ash, and there's nothing you can do about it." Those few words would give me great satisfaction and were the keys to my heart.

We were fighting on the phone one day about his new hook-up, and I screamed at him in my usual manner, "Just tell me you don't love me and I'll walk away!"

He replied angrily, without missing a beat, "I don't love you, Ash." Then he reneged and hastily added, "I don't love you like I used to."

It was as if somebody had stabbed me in the heart with a knife and twisted it.

I gasped and replied, "What?"

The phone went dead. I tried to ring back, but it had been switched off. I stood in the middle of the street, frozen, and began to cry hysterically, screaming out, "No! No! No!" while repeatedly trying to call him. I was pathetic.

Then, as God is my witness, I suddenly heard a voice over my shoulder say, "Wake up to yourself, Ashlee." I looked behind me – there was nobody there. A chill ran down my spine and my shoulders shook. It was like I had just shaken Ronny from my being for the last time.

In that moment, I believe I let go of him completely.

Seventeen

Choices

I refused to see or speak to Ronny for nearly a year. During this time, I underwent extensive counselling to overcome my addiction to him. It was the first time I fully acknowledged what had been happening to me and I called it by its true name: domestic violence.

One day out of the blue Axil asked me if he could live with his father. He was seventeen years old. I was shocked. My initial response was a firm, "No." I questioned him relentlessly on why he would want to go to Collarenebri to live with his father – the man had barely seen or spoken to his son for an entire twelve months. Axil was persistent. It was frustrating. He would say things like, "If you don't let me go, I'll get myself into trouble".

I just didn't know what to do. The reality was he didn't really need my permission. Legally he could go and live with his father.

I asked him one last time, "Why?"

Axil replied, "I just want to be with my dad."

I felt that if I didn't allow him to go, he would hold it against me for the rest of my life. I gave in on the condition that he finish Year 12 and his Higher School Certificate. Once he decided to go, there was no turning back and I began making the arrangements.

It was also time to face my fears – I had to speak to Ronny. I felt I had healed enough to be able to communicate with him. It wasn't easy, but I was willing to do it for my son's sake.

When the day came for Axil to travel to Collarenebri, everything in my being was screaming, *Don't let him go! Don't do it!* But the situation was out of my control. I had convinced myself that he needed to be with his dad so he could learn how to 'be a man'. I knew that it sounded ridiculous, because I certainly didn't want my son to be anything like his father, and yet there we were.

This is a mistake that many women make, especially with their sons. We don't know how to be men, so we think that we can't teach our sons how to be men. We think that our sons need their fathers to show them how to become a man, even if they aren't good fathers, or good men for that matter. What we as mothers need to know is that we are raising good people, regardless of gender.

Thank goodness Ronny's family were responsible because he certainly wasn't. He didn't even have the capacity to enrol his son into school. It was as if he thought that somehow he and I were going to get back together because we were communicating again. He would try to start arguments and tell me what to do, but I refused to play into the old games.

To avoid talking to Ronny, at 4pm every afternoon I would ring his cousin who worked at the school to see how Axil was going. Axil appeared to be doing well, but his father not so much. It turned out that Axil and Ronny didn't get along very well, and one day engaged in a fist fight.

Apparently, Ronny's new girlfriend was becoming jealous of the amount of time Axil was spending with his father. She started a big argument and Axil responded, saying, "He's my dad. Don't tell me what I can and can't do with him!" Apparently, Ronny took his girlfriend's side, and Axil ended up hitting him and nearly knocking him out. They both ended up in tears. I told Axil he should return home, but he insisted there was no need to, that he and his father were fine.

A few weeks later, just half a term short of finishing his HSC, Axil called me to tell me he was leaving school and coming home. My heart sank. I tried to convince him to stay just to finish his HSC, but he wouldn't have a bar of it. He was done. He had made the decision to throw in the towel and come home. Axil also told me he was bringing his girlfriend Krystal to Sydney with him. I said that would be okay.

Krystal was a lovely girl. She was extremely shy and tiny. She was a pretty girl with big brown eyes, her hair was dark brown and went down to her waist, and she had a nice big smile with full lips. It took a few weeks, but she eventually started feeling comfortable around Alyssa and me.

Axil's eighteenth birthday was coming up and we were all excited and busy arranging it. I organised to have his party at the sailing club in Tempe.. It was a great night surrounded by friends and family. Ronny didn't make it as he was back in jail for assault – he had stabbed his new girlfriend's uncle in the head with scissors. I calculated that he had only been present for six of Axil's birthdays.

A few weeks after his birthday, Axil started a horticulture traineeship with a garden nursery and began hanging out with some new mates. He had returned from Collarenebri to Sydney with a bit of an attitude and a chip on his shoulder.

One night, he and his new mates were on their way home from the pub when they decided to rob a man. They took his wallet and ran. The incident was caught on camera.

I have always told Axil that if the police ever picked him up, to always tell the truth. When the police identified Axil in the footage and asked him if it was indeed him, he said, "Yes." However, he insisted he didn't take the wallet and refused to name the other boys who were with him. By identifying himself, he had put himself at the scene of the crime. The police released him and we thought the matter was over, but it wasn't. A few days later the police came to my house. Axil wasn't home yet and they asked me if I knew where he was, but I didn't. Just then Axil walked through the gates, and four police officers approached him.

He turned to me with fear in his eyes and called out, "Mum," looking at me to help him, as if somehow I had the power to make it all better.

I said, "Just walk inside, son."

The arresting officer said, "No," and all four of them surrounded him. They were being a bit rough, so I said to them, "That'll do. Be gentle with him." Instead, they handcuffed him.

I said, "Are you for real? Four police officers for one boy?"

One of the officers turned to me and spat out, "He's not a boy."

If looks could kill, he would have been dead.

I asked where they were taking him, and they told me the police station in. I got into my car and followed the police all the way. When I got inside the police station, they had put him into a holding cell. A short time later, they took him to an interview room. I wasn't allowed in as he was considered an adult because he was eighteen. Axil refused to tell the police who the other boys were. I was furious and I asked the constable if he would let me see him for a minute or two so I could talk some sense into him. What I really wanted to do was slap some sense into him, but they refused.

The officer in charge had the option to give Axil bail, which he did, and I was able to take my son home on the condition that he report to Marrickville Police Station the next day before 3pm. We were all relieved.

The next day, Axil did as he was supposed to and checked in at the police station. He began to walk home and just reached the top of our street when police cars screeched up from all directions and the police arrested him. Krystal was with him at the time. She ran down the road, terrified and screaming to me, "Quick, quick, Ashlee, the police have got Axil!"

I marched straight to the station to see what the hell was going on. They advised me he had been taken to Newtown Police Station's holding cells, so I dashed over there. It turned out the police had decided to charge him. They advised me he would not be leaving the cells that day.

Newtown holding cells are awful. They are cold and dirty, and you can feel the despair in the walls. I was allowed to visit Axil for ten minutes.

We had to sit across from each other, and I wasn't allowed to touch him. My heart broke the very instant our eyes met, but I knew I had to keep myself together, and now was not the time for tears or a lecture. He looked at me with tears in his eyes – my beautiful, perfect son. Since he was a little boy, I had told him it was okay to cry. I had always told him to just tell the truth and all would be okay. Yet here he was, trapped in a dirty cell, surrounded by seasoned criminals. My heart ached and it took everything I had not to break down and cry about what I was about to say next. In order to protect him, I had to tell him to do the exact opposite of what I had taught him; I was about to give him the most difficult advice I ever had to give.

My baby boy looked at me, shoulders slouched with tears streaming down his face and asked, "What do I do, Mum? Tell me what to do."

With every ounce of courage and authority I had in me, I looked him directly in the eye and said, "Stop it. Stop crying like a little bitch. Those other blokes in here will smell your fear from a mile away."

Axil looked at me, shocked. He wiped his eyes and pulled his shoulders back.

I was thankful my son was a big boy. He stood 195 centimetres and weighed about 110 kilos, so if need be he could handle himself.

I then said, "You have to be staunch. Do as you're told. Don't backchat. As soon as you get to jail, go straight to the older Aboriginal men in there and tell them you're Ronny's son. You tell everyone who asks that you're Ronny Stone's son."

He looked at me, surprised. It was the hardest thing I have ever had to tell my son. I knew he would be fine once he got to the jail. His father had done enough jail time to be a somebody in the prison system, even though he was pretty much a nobody in the real world.

I reassured him he would be fine and then my time was up. I wasn't allowed to give him a cuddle. All I could do was tell him I loved him and that everything would be okay.

I ran up the stairs as fast as I could. I just needed to get out as I was holding on by a thread. I couldn't breathe, and as soon as I pushed through the big glass door and stepped outside, the evening air hit my face like a slap. I dropped to my knees, not to pray but because my legs could no longer hold me up. I gasped and let out a terrible scream. It was all I could do. It felt like everything was spinning. I couldn't believe what had just happened. I couldn't believe my only son was in jail. I couldn't believe he was just like his father, because he wasn't – he was MY son.

I don't know how I drove home because I was so distraught and couldn't stop crying. I had never felt so sad in my life. I went into my room, locked the door and sobbed and sobbed. It was as if I had been 'gutted like a yellowbelly', just like Ronny had once threatened me. My heart ached and I fell to the floor and wept some more with my body nearly convulsing. When I had no more tears left, I continued to shake and then I heard a voice – the same voice I had heard once before. "Wake up to yourself, Ashlee, you're no good to anyone in this state. It's time to sort yourself out. Get up and get a grip."

Then, just like that, I stopped. I took a deep breath, pulled myself up off the floor and had a shower. I then took two headache tablets and went to bed.

I woke the next morning with my heart still aching, but I had a different mental perspective. I had a realisation that there was nothing I could do at that moment to get Axil out of the situation he was in. I just had to do what I had always done when his father went to jail. This time, though, I wasn't going to be the best jail wife. Instead, I vowed to be the best jail mum ever, even if this meant speaking to his father.

I took a deep breath and called Ronny to advise him of our son's situation, and he became so upset that it actually shocked me. I don't recall much of the conversation, as we were both blubbering fools. It wasn't even a week before I received a phone call from Ronny, who had breached his parole and was back in jail. He told me he did this deliberately because it gave him a better chance of protecting his son. It was Ronny being the best father he could be in this particular situation. As sad and absurd as this may sound, it gave me great relief and comfort, and I was actually grateful for Ronny.

I attended every court appearance, visited Axil every weekend, made phone calls to ensure he was okay and put money into his bank so he wouldn't go without. At first he was in Long Bay with the older men. I preferred that he was with the old heads as I knew they didn't put up with any nonsense and he would be looked after.

It was during this time that one of my biggest fears surfaced. I had somehow deluded myself into believing that my children would be unaffected by the violence within the family. Because the majority of violent episodes hadn't happened in our home or around the kids, in my blindness I had thought they had been shielded from harm, but nothing could have been further from the truth. I was soon to learn the full extent of the damage that my addiction to Ronny had on the children.

A short while later, we attended Axil's bail hearing at the Supreme Court. His solicitor came over to talk to my mother and me. He advised us he had spoken to Axil about his childhood and was giving me the heads up so I wouldn't be shocked by Axil's answers in the courtroom. He had apparently asked if Axil had been witness or subjected to any domestic violence when he was growing up.

Axil answered, "No, I never saw Dad hit Mum, but one night when we lived at the hostel, I woke up and saw Mum covered in blood."

I felt the blood drain from my face. The solicitor must have seen this because he immediately grabbed my arm and asked if I was okay. I looked at Mum and started crying. I had never felt so guilty in my life. I had put my babies through this because of my own selfishness, and that's just what it was. I hadn't considered anyone else's feelings – not those of my children, my family, my friends or my workmates. If Ronny and I had an episode, I expected everyone to feel sorry for me and to help me, and they always did. As soon as I was ready to forgive Ronny, I expected them to do the same as well, even when he was an arsehole to them. It's a wonder that they stayed around me, and it's no wonder that my son ended up in jail.

This is why I call my all-consuming obsession and dysfunctional love for Ronny an addiction. As most people know, when you're addicted to anything, be it drugs, alcohol, gambling or sex, you don't care about the people around you, and you don't care who you hurt. You just want your fix. I had clearly demonstrated this with my behaviour towards Ronny. I was addicted to him – he was my drug of choice!

My darling son was subsequently moved from jail to jail. I repeatedly asked my mother to do something, but she kept saying that she couldn't. She wasn't allowed to help him because they were related. I didn't care about this, nor could I get my head around it. I remember screaming at her once, "For fuck's sake, help him! He's your grandson," not fully understanding that the implications of my demands would not only jeopardise her job, but also put them both in danger.

They finally stopped moving him around after I had been advised to contact the Manager of Indigenous Classification and point out that my son was a first-timer, only eighteen years old and Aboriginal. I knew through the Royal Commission into Aboriginal Deaths in Custody that moving my son around would put him at high risk, so Corrective Services eventually brought him back to Long Bay.

His hearing was ridiculous. People were getting bail for attempted murder and rape but he was knocked back for 'robbery in company' charge.

I was so thankful during this time for Ronny's cousin Jack. He stayed with me and attended every court hearing. He didn't have to, he just did. His support was unwavering, and he was the only person who stood by me throughout the entire experience. He didn't falterI'll be forever grateful for his loyalty to us.

As it turned out, 2009 was an extremely difficult year for me. As well as the fact that my son was in jail, I was looking after two nieces who had been removed from their parents by the Department of Community Services. Alyssa was also starting Year 11, so I needed to ensure she didn't miss out on my attention. My nieces were just babies; one was three months old and the other had just turned one. I had to work around their schedule for my weekly jail visits. Thank goodness for my daughter and Krystal's help, otherwise I wouldn't have been able to cope.

There was a lot of family drama surrounding the girls, too. They weren't allowed to leave Sydney and no one else's house was appropriate, so I offered to take them in. I figured if my grandmother had raised eleven of her own children, helped with her grandchildren and great-grandchildren, and none of them had been taken away, then I wasn't about to break the pattern. I didn't think too much about the consequences or the impact that this decision would have on my life. I just did it because in my eyes it was the right thing to do, and I'd do it again in a heartbeat.

It was during this time that my best friend Bella and I made a pact to travel to New York City for New Year's Eve. I don't remember where the idea came from or how it was going to happen, but I held onto it for dear life. It was this dream that helped me navigate the most difficult year of my life.

I started to pray every night and began attending a Saturday meditation class. At this point in my life, these two practices were my only 'me' time.

I also decided to start reading books again. One day at work I picked up a book from our donations library. It was a small, unassuming book that appeared from nowhere. I turned it over to read the back and thought, *This book looks familiar*. Just then I remembered it was the same book my Aunty May had given me years ago when I was working at the day care centre. She was the first woman I had witnessed being violently assaulted, by her husband Thomas.

It was a Friday afternoon and I was at my aunty and uncle's house. They lived up the road from us in Kempsey at the time. I loved them both and sometimes I would think, *I hope I'm as happily married as them one day*.

On this particular day, however, Aunty May was late getting home from work. My uncle was in happy spirits, and his eldest daughter Carla and I started to prepare dinner.

As my aunty walked in the front door she too was in good spirits, talking about how successful the meeting she just attended had been. Before she could say another word, my uncle leaped up from the couch, took off his belt and dragged her down the hallway to the backyard where he began beating her with the strap and his fists. I could hear her screaming, "I'm sorry, please stop. No, no, no!"

Then my uncle appeared again in the hall. He instructed his daughters to go and see to their mother. I stood there frozen, and then quickly and quietly ran home.

I stayed away for a couple of days and then built up the courage to visit my aunty. She was sitting in the lounge with a cloth nappy wrapped around her head. I sat on the arm of the chair and put my arm around her. She looked up at me and said, "I told him if he ever hits me again, I'll leave." I put my head softly on hers and nodded.

I was fourteen years old.

I don't think he ever hit her again – not to my knowledge anyway. Several years later when I was twenty-three, Aunty May gave me the book *Women Who Love Too Much* by Robin Norwood. At the time, I couldn't understand why she thought I needed to read this book. I opened it and read a few pages but just couldn't get into it.

It took nearly twenty years before I was ready to read it, and once I started I didn't stop. I read it within a day. The relief I felt finding out I wasn't the only one experiencing this situation was life changing. My senses were reawakened. I wanted more, so I bought several self-help books, such as *Don't Call That Man* by Rhonda Findling. Then I saw an episode of Oprah dedicated to Rhonda Byrne's book *The Secret.* Something stirred in me and, like so many others, I went in search of my authentic self. The knowledge I found in those books led me towards a new way of viewing the world, life, family and myself.

It was also around this time I became involved in a research proposal led by Mudgin-Gal Aboriginal Corporation. The research project's aim was to identify how different age groups of Aboriginal women identify and deal with domestic violence. We were assisted in the research by academic, social commentator and feminist Eva Cox. I loved researching, and I loved the way Eva thought and put things into perspective. It was Eva who gave me the tools to identify and learn the most valuable lesson of my life.

One day we gathered into our groups and, as usual, I had a lot to share. I was only just starting to speak openly about my experience with domestic violence without crying. However, I wasn't quite ready to share my experience of having an eighteen-year-old son in jail. Having said that, I also knew I had to move through the pain. Then Eva posed a question to me.

She asked, "Ashlee, if you knew at the time that staying in a relationship with Ronny for as long as you did would eventually lead to your son Axil ending up in jail, would you have stayed?"

I immediately said, "No, of course not."

Eva looked at me and just smiled. It wasn't until I got home that night, fixed the girls up and settled in, that the full impact of what Eva had asked hit me.

By staying with Ronny and supporting him in and out of jail, I was in fact teaching my son that it was okay to become a criminal and to be incarcerated. I had also normalised the situation by visiting Ronny and constantly providing him with money. My children and I probably visited every jail in New South Wales, so I was teaching Axil and Alyssa that jail was a normal part of life and not to be scared because Mummy would look after them. At this realisation, I had another breakdown or – depending on the perspective – a breakthrough! Either way, I was never the same again. I knew I had to take responsibility for my part in Axil ending up in jail.

The next day Axil called. I knew it was now or never. It was finally time to take responsibility. As we were chatting I said, "Axil, you know I love you and I know you love me. I need to tell you I'm SO sorry, my baby, for teaching you it's okay to go to jail, when in reality it's not."

He didn't interrupt. He just listened.

Then he said ever so softly, "It's okay, Mum, we'll get through this."

My son – my beautiful, perfect boy who had been through so much – assured me that all would be okay. I thanked him for being such a good son and helping me to learn the most valuable lesson in my life.

Until we take responsibility for our part in any behaviour that we interpret as either negative or positive, we can never move forwards – we become stuck. I was stuck for years because I allowed myself to be treated so badly. It wasn't just Ronny it was me, too. Taking responsibility for your actions and decisions is the first step in moving up a level in life. I'm not saying it's easy, and most of the time these realisations hurt immensely, but it is necessary in order to truly live a life of substance. We have to take responsibility for everything we do.

The one thing that got me through the difficult year was my dream of spending New Year's Eve in New York City. I held onto this dream with all my might.

The girls' grandmother, my Aunty Angie, came down to help look after my two nieces. This was a relief to me as I was barely keeping my head above water. Eventually, after an intense legal battle, Angie became the permanent carer for the girls and they all happily moved back home to Kempsey. This wasn't as easy as it sounded, but it all worked out in the end.

Axil was finally sentenced. He received a twelve-month jail term, but thank goodness it included the time he had already served. I advised him that I would never set foot into a jail or a courthouse again. I had spent half my life doing that, and I refused to spend the next half doing the same thing. The first time it's a mistake; the second time it's a choice. It was time I got on with my life. I couldn't change the past, but I learned I could create my future.

Eighteen

Step by Step

It turned out my friend Bella wasn't able to fly to New York with me. But nothing was going to stop me. I had never been so determined to accomplish anything in my life. I didn't want to go alone, so I asked my Aunty Cynthia if she would come with me and she agreed. I busied myself by organising the accommodation, tours and flights.

We boarded our flight on 30 December 2009. My life was about to step up a notch. I was so excited I could barely sit still and all I could think was, *Wow, I did it! I'm going to New York!* One would assume that after a seventeen-hour trip, my excitement would have subsided – but it didn't.

After going through customs and immigration, we stepped into a cold, snowy evening and I felt ecstatic. It was like I had been electrocuted, in a good way. I didn't even feel the cold. We jumped into our first yellow cab and drove off to our motel.

We arrived and checked into our room, which was perfect. We were too excited to sleep, so we decided to go for a wander and get something to eat. I'll never forget the feeling of walking down a New York street for the first time. It was like I was in Michael Jackson's 'Billie Jean' film clip; each time I took a step, the footpath lit up. I fell in love with New York instantly.

We stumbled over to Times Square, which was only a few blocks from where we were staying. Oh my goodness, we didn't know where to start looking. We stood on the side of the street, where images of pedestrians are projected onto a giant screen. We took photos of ourselves on the screen and walked around a bit more. There was so much to see and do. New York had indeed earned its reputation as 'the city that never sleeps'.

We decided to try a New York pizza and couldn't believe we could buy two slices for a dollar! If money became tight, we knew what we'd be eating. We returned to our motel and settled in for the night. The next day was New Year's Eve, as well as my forty-first birthday.

We woke just before lunch. *Shit!* I thought, *we've slept half the day away*. We quickly got ready and headed to Macy's. I couldn't get enough of all the sights and sounds: the yellow cabs, the police and ambulance sirens, the biggest billboard I ever saw with a half-naked David Beckham on it, the different hats and wigs, and shops … gosh, there were shops everywhere. I was in awe. Thankfully, Aunty Cynthia had a good sense of direction, otherwise we would have got lost.

We reached Macy's and strolled through every floor. I had never seen a department store like it. We were told when we got there to go to level one to get a twenty per cent discount card for visitors, which we did. That was the easy part. Attempting to navigate through Macy's for the first time was hectic, to say the least. The lifts were old, wooden and creaky, so we opted for the escalators. We eventually found the floor that sold women's winter jackets.

We had only ventured in to buy warm coats, but three hours later we emerged carrying a mountain of bags. We headed back to our motel and stumbled across a quaint little restaurant called Tick Tock. It was like a *Happy Days* set and we fell in love with it so it became our regular food joint.

We had a little rest at the motel and sorted ourselves out for the upcoming evening. We were going on a New Year's Eve cruise. We dolled up in our new jackets and were ready to roll. We hailed a yellow cab and drove to our destination. When we arrived, we realised we were at the wrong pier. We asked for directions and it took us about ten minutes to walk to the right location.

We were both excited, although I think my excitement was completely off the charts compared to Cynthia's. She would look at me occasionally, shake her head and smile.

The boat was nice and warm, and decorated beautifully. We were given 2010 champagne flutes and princess tiaras along with pretty beads and blow horns. The alcohol flowed and the food came out. They served king prawns, chicken skewers, meatballs and oysters. The drinks were free and plentiful, and Cynthia and I mingled, made some friends, and danced. We had the best time!

The new year was looming. I needed a moment, so I walked out onto the deck, completely overwhelmed with emotion and reflecting on all I had been through during the previous years.

Then the countdown began: 10, 9, 8 … it started to snow as we sailed past the Statue of Liberty … 3, 2, 1, and then the fireworks exploded.

Happy New Year!

I started to cry with happiness. I spoke softly to myself through my sobs, "You did it!"

A realisation came over me that there was nothing I couldn't do if I put my mind to it. If I could make it here, I could make it anywhere … New York! New York!

Happy New Year! Happy, happy New Year!

For the first time in over twenty years, it really was a Happy New Year.

Epilogue

Wounds into Wisdom

Since my forty-first birthday, I have undertaken extensive healing – mentally, physically, emotionally and spiritually. I came to the realisation that in order to move forwards, I had to take responsibility for my actions, and in order to accomplish this, I had to navigate through the pain of my past. I couldn't go around it or over it, I had to walk through it. I'm not going to say it was easy, because it wasn't – it was uncomfortable and torturous at times. But it was nothing compared to the misery I had lived through, so I decided to turn my wounds into wisdom and consequently became an advocate for the anti-violence message.

Education, again, helped me to heal. I graduated from the University of Technology Sydney with a Master of Education, and won the UTS Human Rights Award.

Before I could do this, I needed to allow myself to heal. I sought counselling, but in all honesty I didn't ever think counselling was a good idea, as I couldn't see the benefit. It took me three attempts with different counsellors to find the right one for me. On my first attempt, I only attended one session. I had a male counsellor who made me feel uneasy from the get go, as at that point in time I was not ready to 'start from the beginning' – my childhood – as he insisted. I was barely able to come to terms with my domestic violence experience let alone delve into the murky waters of my childhood. I didn't return.

My second experience wasn't much better. She was an older woman who seemed nice for the first fifteen minutes, then she asked me to visualise Ronny as a pillow in the corner and suggested that I punch into it! I thought, *What? Is she mad?* Again, this was enough to turn me off completely, and so I never returned. It took me another year to muster up the courage to attend counselling again. I knew I needed to speak to someone who didn't know me, or my story and who wouldn't judge me … I just needed someone to vent to, and I finally found him. My third counsellor was a young man fresh out of university. He knew nothing about me and not a lot about Aboriginal people either – especially women. However, this didn't matter because I was there to heal, to get in touch with my feelings and release them. I stayed with him for over two years, and I will be forever indebted to him. I believe we helped each other, as I was one of his first clients. We grew and learned together, and he gave me some valuable tools that I still use to this day.

I didn't participate in any further counselling for a few years, however I started exploring my spiritual side, attending Kundalini yoga, learning to meditate, and reading self-help books by the dozen. I also started to be drawn to like-minded women – women who themselves survived and thrived, and women who to this day are in my close-knit circle of friends. Each and every one of them have instilled in me the belief that I matter; they hear me, they see me, and they let me be me. To surround ourselves with people who nourish our souls is so important in the journey of healing.

After a few years, I felt I still needed more counselling, more to deal with my sexual abuse than the domestic violence. This became apparent when I began to work with Rape and Domestic Violence Services Australia where I was fortunate enough to be provided with 'self-care', which led me to the therapist I credit with helping me more than any person in my life. She became my confidant for my life, for my dreams and for my deepest darkest secrets. I still see her every now and then to this day, and whenever I need an outlet I go to her.

Another great healer for me was education. I went back to university with the encouragement of my senior lecturer, who is one of the smartest women I know. She is an Aboriginal woman who has achieved so much through education, and is truly one of my biggest influences around the benefits of learning. I always liked learning, and all I needed was encouragement. Without her insistence and encouragement I would never have gone to university, never graduated and never taught. And so, I graduated from the University of Technology Sydney (UTS) with a Master of Education in Indigenous Studies and won the UTS Human Rights Award.

After my healing through counselling, education and the work that I was being directed to do, I started to talk about the story of my experience, and this too was a form of healing. Doing this led me down the path of becoming an educator for the anti-violence movement. I produced training materials for the schools' component of the award-winning Tackling Violence program aimed at men, using rugby league as a vehicle to spread the anti-violence message to men, women and high school students. I have also trained male ambassadors to be able to deliver this program, and presented at over one hundred schools and provided education on domestic violence to over a thousand men, women and high school students in country New South Wales.

I was the lead writer for the national domestic violence education kit 'Voice Against Violence' for Australia's National Rugby League. I have trained and presented to some of our most prominent and successful rugby league players, produced the training manual, trained the trainers and facilitated workshops. I have also developed programs for young women with a focus on domestic violence education and healthy relationships. I am the co-creator, alongside Dixie Link-Gordon, of the only Aboriginal women's sexual assault network in Australia called 'Hey Sis, we'vewe've got your back', in conjunction with Rape and Domestic Violence Services Australia.

During this period of growth, Dixie and I were advised by a supporter of the service we were working for that we should attend the United Nations Commission on the Status of Women forum in New York City. When Dixie spoke to me about this it sent tingles up my spine. I had already been to New York and loved it, and I thought, *To have the opportunity to attend a forum that fights for the rights of women worldwide would be amazing*. So, we got to work. We had to raise our own funds and go through a strenuous process to be accredited to attend. We had so many setbacks it wasn't funny.

Then one day, we were trying to 'sell' our plight to a non-Aboriginal woman who was fairly high up in the spectrum of the anti-violence movement. She said, "Why do you two want to go to THAT forum, shouldn't you be going to the forum for Indigenous people?"

I looked at her, then at Dixie and said, "Why wouldn't we want to go? We are WOMEN, proud Aboriginal women who have a voice and an opinion on what Aboriginal women go through, want and need."

She looked at me, shrugged her shoulders and dismissed us. My blood was boiling. I looked at Dixie and told her that we were going to go to this forum. For far too long now non-Aboriginal women have been telling us what is best for us, so it was time we took a stand at an international level.

I swear, as soon as we made up our minds that we were worthy of attending, and realised that our voices mattered, the floodgates opened. People started saying yes to sponsoring us, and we were put onto one woman who seemed to have the magic key to every door. We did it – we got there! We engaged, we learned and it was amazing. Since that first forum we have now presented at the United Nations Commission on the Status of Women forum in New York City on five occasions. Dixie and I have presented on topics such as urban Aboriginal women's voices around domestic violence and sexual assault, the Tackling Violence program, and the 'Hey Sis, we've got your back' network. I have also spoken about my individual experiences and work around the anti-domestic violence message, which led me to write this book. My first visit was one of my proudest moments, and the determination and passion that drove us has been a major influence into shaping the woman I am today.

I have spoken and presented at numerous conferences as well as on radio and television around the anti-violence message in Australia. I also featured as one of one hundred people in the Positively Remarkable People: Ending Violence Against Women' exhibition, a collection of photographic portraits and stories of individuals and groups based in Sydney. I was also one of ten Indigenous women in the Amnesty International Australia 'Celebrating Indigenous Mums' feature.

Most recently, I have supported the adaptation and contextualisation of an international intimate partner violence curriculum for the Australian Nurse-Family Partnership Program (ANFPP) to maximise the understanding of domestic and family violence for ANFPP staff working in the Indigenous community/primary healthcare area.

I share these experiences in hope that if you are reading this and have thought about counselling but decided it's not for you – or like me, you had some bad experiences – you will be encouraged not to give up. You will find the right one for you, and when you do your whole world will change. Counselling has been one of my biggest healers and I recommend it to anyone.

When telling my story, I encourage people to find something they love, or even like, and to do it. The healing that comes with completing or accomplishing something you have set your mind to is so beneficial, and if you think it's going to take too long, always remember that the time will pass anyway, so utilise it.

When we leave any abusive relationship, there is a void in our lives and we run the risk of allowing ourselves to become bored because the space that our partners once filled is now empty. We need to fill that space with beneficial tasks, or we run the risk of returning to these people out of 'loneliness'. Fill the void with activities, learning, exercise, music, art, meditation – anything that fills your heart, mind, body and soul. For me, my top three were education, travel and counselling. In 2013, the course of my life changed when I was selected to attend a writer's retreat in Bali after applying through an advert that popped up on my Facebook feed. I was one of thirteen people to be chosen from applicants around the WORLD – one of thirteen!!! I lived and worked there for thirty days with other participants and Mastin Kipp – founder of The Daily Love – and wrote my book. The rest, as they say, is history.

My children have grown into respectful, loving adults who are now both parents themselves.

My beloved grandmother passed away in 1999 – my heart still aches.

My mother is still working, and we have a wonderful relationship.

My sister has married the love of her life and is living in America.

I still speak to all my aunties and uncles in a loving and respectful manner.

George is still one of my dearest friends.

Bella and I no longer talk. I'm unsure why and it still hurts my heart today.

Ronny is still in and out of jail, battling his demons with addiction and abusing women.

And ME? Well, I'm living the LIFE!

Audrey Hepburn once said, "Nothing is impossible, even the word spells 'I'm possible'".

I'm living proof of this. Don't give up, don't you ever give up.

You got this!

ACKNOWLEDGEMENTS

There are many people to thank for helping me bring this book to life.

Firstly, my children they are the loves of my life and my greatest accomplishments.

My mother, for instilling in me resilience, and loving me unconditionally.

My grandmother and great-grandmother – two of the most pivotal women in my life.

My sister, for her unwavering support and love. Ronny for giving me the gift of motherhood.

Bella and George, for being the best friends I ever had.

Dixie Link-Gordon, for being my sounding board for the hard stories I had to tell, and for her unwavering belief and support throughout the whole writing process.

Anita Heiss for encouraging me to write this damn book, and for her constant advice, time and guidancc throughout.

Tammy Solonec, if it wasn't for her, I'm not sure I would have finished.

Julie Ditrich, for making my words dance off the pages. The universe works in wonderful ways.

Wirringa Baiya Aboriginal Women's Legal Centre for the generous support throughout this process.

Mastin Kipp and Jill Esplin for providing me with the opportunity, space and mentorship throughout the Daily Love Writers' Retreat in Bali, to take my book out of my mind and onto the page. I will be forever grateful.

Pat Verducci, my Bali writing mentor – if I didn't have her while I was writing this book, I may have crumbled.

Kelly Notoras, whose generosity, kindness and support allowed me to believe I could do it … and I have.

My Bali sisters – Cheryl, Erin, Jamie, Kamina, Kat, Katie, Liz, Megan, Sarah and Tara. Special mention to Kate – the first person to read my manuscript – for her time, love and support. What a journey. Thank you all for allowing me to just be me.

And last but not least, my woohoo sister Sapna Prasad … Wow. I am so glad she came into my life … that is all.

To all who I have crossed paths with over the years – thank you. There have been many lessons, all of which I am grateful for.

COMPELLING READS
FROM MAGABALA

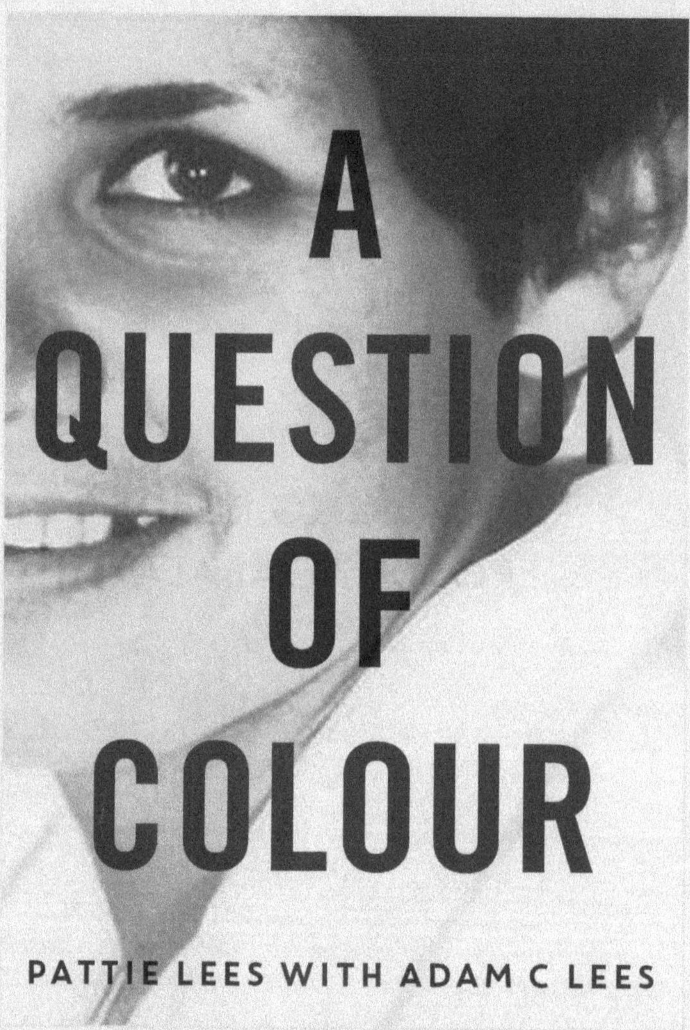

PRAISE FOR A QUESTION OF COLOUR

"In Pattie Lees' memoir...words reveal the grace and emotional transcendence the author has undoubtedly reached as a survivor of the stolen generations. Lees combines history and memoir with such tact, delicacy and reverence that for all 334 pages, I felt strengthened by her crisp storytelling."

Jessie Tu

The Sydney Morning Herald

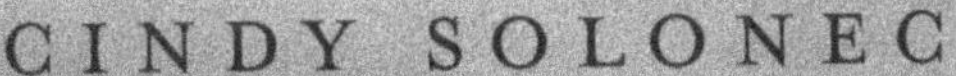

Debesa

The Story of
Frank and Katie Rodriguez

PRAISE FOR DEBESA

"...full of heart and humour...A triumph of the book is the characters that infuse it with life."

DC White

GLAM Adelaide

THE

BOY FROM BIRDUM

BILL DEMPSEY

WITH STEVE HAWKE

PRAISE FOR THE BOY FROM BIRDUM

"This is an honest and unpretentious story, well-told, that deserves wide readership."

Lionel Frost

Sporting Traditions

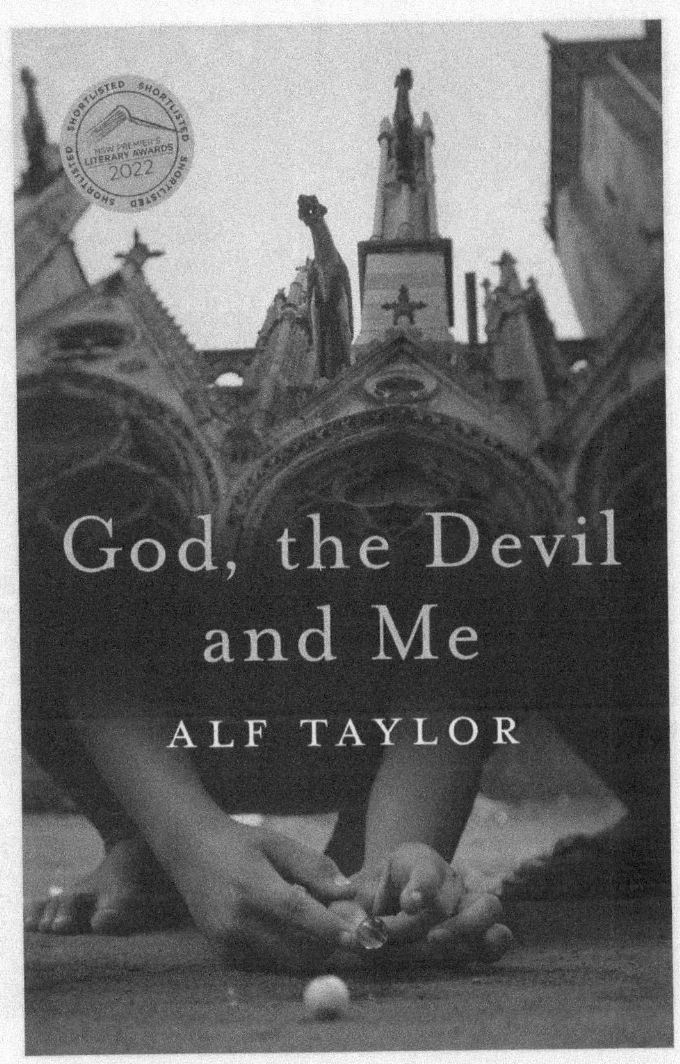

PRAISE FOR GOD, THE DEVIL AND ME

"Taylor has created a private universe...by turns incredibly sad and comic..."

Steven Carroll

The Sydney Morning Herald

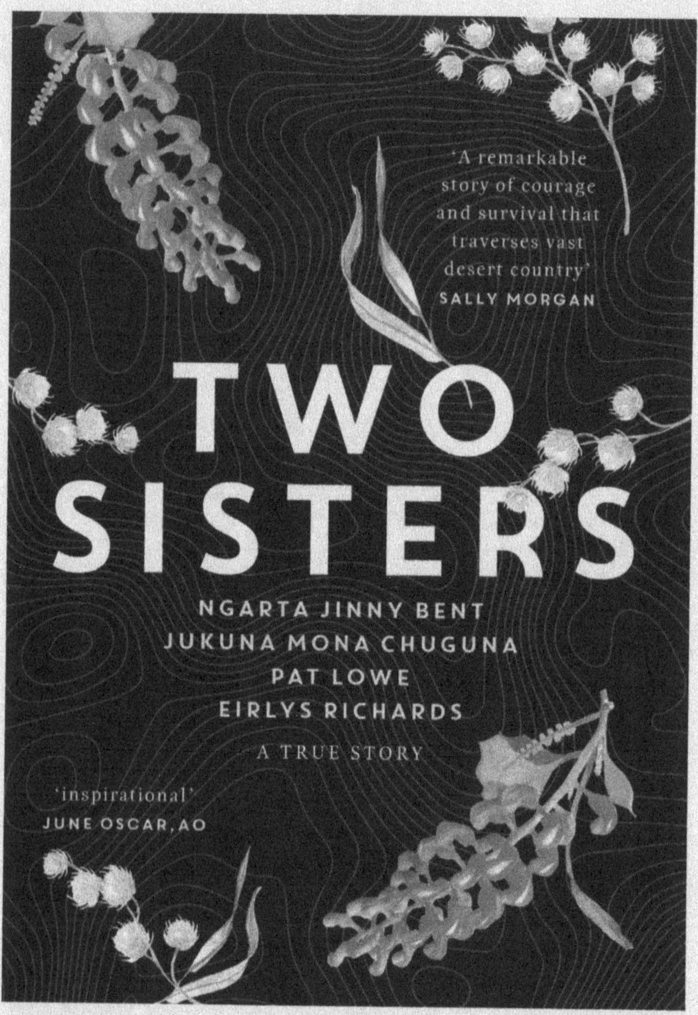

PRAISE FOR TWO SISTERS

"Unwavering courage shouts resolutely from the pages of this lyrical but gutsy true account of two Walmajarri sisters as they are pursued by murderers and face the loss of their ancient lifestyle."

Marie Munkara
Author